ECONOMIC REFORMS AND PUBLIC DISTRIBUTION SYSTEM

ECONOMIC REFORMS AND PUBLIC DISTRIBUTION SYSTEM

Dr. M. Soundarapandian
Reader
Department of Rural Industries and Management
Gandhigram Rural Institute, Deemed University
Gandhigram—624 302
Tamil Nadu

SERIALS PUBLICATIONS
New Delhi

First Published–2003

ISBN: 81-86771-20-4

Published by:

Head Office : **SERIALS PUBLICATIONS**
4, B.S.S. Hall, Khyber Pass Market,
Civil Lines, Delhi–110 054 (India)
Fax: 91-11-23272135
E-mail: serials@satyam.net.in

Branch Office : 4830/24, Prahlad Street, Ansari Road,
Darya Ganj, New Delhi-110002 (India)
Phone: 23245225

Typeset By : *Shankar Bose*

Printed by : R. K. Offset Process,
Naveen Shahdara, Delhi -32

Printed In India

Preface

The main objectives of the New Economic Policy is creating conducive economic environment for promoting sustainable economic growth in the country. The structural reforms comprise measures such as Deregulation, Denationalisation, Deflation, and Devaluation. The Public Distribution System (PDS) in India forms an important strategy for intervening in the distribution of food grains and other essential commodities. The deregulations under economic reforms have influenced the performance of PDS in India.

A number of studies made on PDS have shown that the programme is not doing very well. Besides the prevalent view is that the overemphasis on subsidies under PDS is desirable and it is a major anti poverty programme. With the purpose of studying, the impact of the PDS and performance of PDS in Dindigul District during the period 1986-87 to 1995-96, a project work has been done with the help of the financial assistance under Indian Council of Social Science Research.

My profound thanks are due to Dr. N. Thillai Nayagam, Professor and Head, Department of Rural Industries and Management, Gandhigram Rural Institute, for having encouraged me to undertake this project. The report could not have been published but for the financial assistance by the ICSSR made available for me, under the scheme of support for major research project in the Humanities and Social Sciences, my thanks are due to them.

My thanks are due to Mr. C. Rajkumar, Research Assistant for his assistance in the collection of data and also thanks to My wife Mrs. S. Indhumathi and children B. Dhanalakshmi and S. Vidhya for their support to complete the work.

I would like to acknowledge my debt to the State Trading Corporations, Food and Civil Supplies Department, Chennai, District Supplies Officials, Tamil Nadu Civil Supplies Corporations, Taluk Officials, Block Officials, Municipality Officials of the Dindigul District, and the 300 respondents of the PDS Beneficiaries and non-PDS Beneficiaries who helped us a lot in getting the various data and information for this project.

Dr. M. Soundarapandian

Contents

1

Introduction

Economic Reforms

Several major economic and political influences occurred during the 1970's and 1980's, which affected the developing countries and paved the way for the implementation of IMF-sponsored Structural Adjustment Policies. By the 1970's the development strategies that many post-colonial countries had adopted in order to develop their economies to a high-growth path had started slowing down. This was due to a combination of actors, which differed from country to country, but were mainly resulting from the colonial legacy (stagnant agriculture, low levels of industrialization, inadequate capital), adverse terms of trade in international markets for primary product exporters, and limits to domestic resource mobilization due to a fairly narrow tax-base of high income earners. It was becoming increasingly difficult for these economies to pursue economic development, whether through import-substitution or export-promotion strategies.

The restructuring of the world's financial system which was undertaken at the end of the second world war saw the setting up of the Briton Woods Institutions-the International Monetary Fund (IMF) and the International Bank for Reconstruction and Development (IBRD). The main international policy concerns during the 1950's were post-war reconstruction in the developed countries and post-colonial economic development in the developing countries.

By the early 1970's, however, the situation changed dramatically, fixed exchange rate were abonded and they were allowed to flat as they were no longer pegged to the dollar. The U.S. economy moved to a balance of payments situation of massive of post-war successes like Germany and Japan. With the first sharp rise in International Oil prices in 1973, further changes were set in motion in the worlds financial system as petro-dollars-"hot money"-flowed into developing countries in Search of short-term high-yielding returns. This was one of the contributory factors to the debt crisis in developing countries, which reached alarming proportion especially in Latin America during the 1980's and set the stage for implementing the reform package.

The Collapse of the Soviet Union at the end of the decade further speeded up the rejection of commend-type economic policies and opened up the space for the processes of liberalization and globalization[1]. To restore Macro economic stability, the reforms package of structural adjustment policies are aimed at freeing markets by dismantling controls on production, prices and trade and reducing intervention in the economy. The need to control the fiscal deficit led to policies to curb public expenditure and these cuts were mainly on social sector expenditure and on production and consumption subsidies which directly affected the living standards of the economically vulnerable sections of the population. Privatization, Liberalization, and export-promotion were the main features of the economic reforms recommended by the international institution for the problems facing the developing countries.

At the same, the role of the state in advanced industrial economies was not shirking as expected, but growing despite the ideological bias in favour of a "rolled-back" State. The share of national income spends by government, which averaged 30% in the rich industrial countries in 1960 to 42.5% by 1980 and 45% by 1990[2]. The experience of countries, which have undergone these reforms, has in most cases not led to the expected outcome but has in fact worsened the state of their economies[3].

In India, the New Economic Policy (NEP) is a set of policy (ies) and administrative procedures introduced in July 1991 to bring about changes in the economic direction of the country. It has got two major components stabilization and structural reforms.

Stabilization part has again three components

(i) Management of Balance of payments

(ii) Control of Inflation.

(iii) Fiscal correction.

Structural Reforms part has seven components

(i) Exchange rate adjustment.

(ii) Liberalization of imports.

(iii) Rationalization of tariff structure.

(iv) Delicensing/removal of Licensing restrictions.

(v) Financial sector reforms.

(vi) Disinvestment of public sector shares.

(vii) Foreign Direct Investment.

The congress led Government completed full five years with policies of New Economic Reforms. The United Front Government and BJP led Alliance also carried forward the reform process more or less on the same line as the Congress Government. A synoptic view of the achievement of the economic reforms is given in Table 1.

There was very satisfactory growth rate in GDP since 1991-92. The momentum of growth has been maintained providing increasing evidence that the growth potential has improved as a result of the reforms initiated in 1991. The Eighth Plan (1992-97) ended with an average growth of 6.5 percent per annum. The year 1991-92 was a bad year and if it was excluded, then the growth rate of the economy during the Eighth plan works out to be 6.8 percent per annum, but if 1991-92 is also taken into consideration, then for the 6 years period of economic reform (1991-92 to 1997-98), the growth rate average 5.5 percent. However, there is no doubt that after 1992-93, the economy has picked up and the growth rate reached an average level of 7 percent during the 3 years (1994-95 to 1996-97). This can be considered as a legitimate achievement of the economic reforms. The major issue is to sustain this high growth rate and re-orient the content of growth so that it makes a definite dent on poverty and unemployment.

Another major achievement of the economic reform is the control of inflation. There is no doubt that during 1995-96, there has been decline in the rate of growth of wholesale price index (WPI) to 7.8 percent as against 10.9

Table 1
Key Economic Indicators
(After Economic Liberalization)

Sl. No.		*1990-91*	*1997-98*	*Annual Average Growth rate (1991-1998)*
1.	GDP (1980-81 prices) (Rs thousand crores)	212	311	5.7
2.	Agricultural Production (Index: 1980-81=100.)	148	165	1.5
3.	Foodgrain Production (Million tonnes)	176	192	1.2
4.	Industrial Production (1993-94=100)	92	138	6.0
5.	Wholesale price Index (1981-82=100)	183	337	9.1
6.	Consumer price Index (1982=100)	193	366	9.6
7.	Export (US $ Million)	18,140	33,980	9.4
8.	Imports (US $ Million)	24,070	40,780	7.9
9.	Foreign Exchange Reserve	2,240	25,980	41.9
10.	Rate of Exchange (Rs/US $)	17.9	37.2	10.9

Source: Compiled from Government of India, Economic Survey, 1998-99.

percent during 1994-95. But a broad view of the 7-year's period reveals that the annual average growth rate of WPI was of the order of 9.1 percent during 1990-91 and 1997-98. Since 1996-97 the WPI showed a relatively small increase. These are developments.

A more reliable index, which measures the cost of living, is the consumer price index (CPI). If we take the entire 7-years period, CPI for industrial workers showed annual average rise by 9.6 percent. A near double-digit rise in CPI cover the entire post-reform period has serious welfare implications.

According to the Planning Commission in 1993-94, about 36 percent of the total population (about 320 million) were living below the poverty line. Out of this, 244 million lived in the rural areas and 76 million lived in the urban areas. The poverty percentage for the rural areas was 37.3 and that for urban areas was 32.4. Obviously, economic reforms have not succeeded in making a serious dent on poverty.

The far-reaching changes at the domestic and international levels over the past decade will therefore clearly have an impact on India's agricultural sector. As far as the role of the state in the domestic economic is concerned, Indian economic planning based on the Nehruian model since the early 1950s had given a commanding role to the state to direct and regulate economic activity in all sectors of the economy apart from ownership of economic resources in key sectors. This position has changed in recent years- but with the reduction of the state's role in vulnerable sector like agriculture will be affected in several areas, such as public investments, irrigation development, input subsidies, food security etc.

Though these policies and procedures have a macro-economic thrust, their impact on micro-level economic activities cannot be ignored. From that point of view the new economic policy will have repercussions on the entire game of rural development issues. While discussing these aspects the following points require to be seriously considered.

Firstly the new economic policy was introduced in July 1991 in the wake of a severe foreign exchange crisis faced by the country. The foreign exchange reserves dwindled to mere three weeks requirements and the country appeared headed for a near bankruptcy situation. Immediate recourse to accommodation from IMF became necessary and it is widely perceived that the new economic policy was launched in response to IMF Conditionalities. This aspect weakens the legitimacy and political appeal of the policy in the eyes of the public[4].

Secondly, the reforms followed soon after the assumption of office by a new government, which did not have enough time to take stock of the situation.

Thirdly, going by the record of many countries in Latin America and Africa, structural adjustment didn't succeed in most countries. Even Mexico touted as a success story and a basket case, seriously faltered with the outbreak of peasant rebellion in chiapas province in January 1994 and plight of foreign capital and devaluation of Peso in December 1994. It is no comforting thought that in East Asia and South East Asia, structural adjustment worked. In those countries, sound policies to improve literacy, health care, agrarian relations and economic conditions of the people were undertaken. India is no where these countries, with only 52.1 percent literacy, with much lower levels for rural people, women and scheduled castes, and scheduled tribes, poor health care, high infant morality rate of 80 percent people below poverty line.

Fourthly, the new economic policy does not directly address issues of rural development but many of the policy instruments in the new economic policy will have adverse effect on rural development.

Management of balance of payment will lead to import compression, directly affecting fertilizer imports and export promotion, encouraging export led growth in agriculture ignoring food security. Fiscal correction will lead to expenditure control, leading to reduction of subsidies for fertilizers and food and cut back in outlays in the social sector. Liberalization of import expose 842 products of protected Small Industries to competition from imported goods. Liberalization of licensing producers will also encourage setting up of industrial activities in areas exclusively reserved for protected sectors. Financial sector reforms, with emphasis of prudential norms, will affect credit for rural development schemes. Disinvestment of public sector shares will dilute the social concerns of the public undertakings.

The another issue relates to the international dimension of opening up the economy to global market forces. The conclusion of the Uruguay Round of trade talks with the Marrakech Agreement of 14 has altered the framework of multinational trade. This is likely to have a series of effects on domestic prices of agricultural commodities, their production levels, crop patterns and the viability of the more vulnerable small and marginal farms. With the entry of Multinational Companies (MNCs) into export-oriented agriculture, the threat of dispossession of small and marginal farmers is a serious factor[6].

Subsidies are given to different sections of population and sectors by taking into account the need for incentive and welfare of the people as well. Incentives are given to boost the production; subsidies are also given to the people to improve the quality life. Subsidies are given for different sectors like Agriculture, industry, and service including education and health. Subsidies are given in almost all countries all over the world. India is no exception to it[7].

Majority of people in the rural areas is small and marginal farmers, agricultural labourers, rural artisans and others, who are poor by any known standards. Even today 39 percent of the people are below poverty line. In order to provide them a reasonable quantum of food for consumption, the food items such as rice, wheat, vegetable oils, kerosene, sugar are supplied to the people at subsidized price through public distribution system. An amount of Rs. 5000 crores is allocated for food subsidy in the 1993-94 central budget.

It is felt that the allocation of funds for public distribution system is grossly inadequate in view of the vast majority of poor people living all over the country. Under these circumstances, the proposal for withdrawal of subsidies on food, as suggested by International Financing Institutions, comes as a bolt from blue. It is feared that the government will be forced to implement this suggestion. If the suggestion is put into practice it will directly hit the poorer sections of the people, who will die of hunger, undernourishment and malnutrition.

The fact that the new economic policy, particularly the subsidy withdrawal, globalization, privatization and foreign investment into our country will adversely affect the agricultural production and will damage the food security system, education, health and other services will be inaccessible to poor people. The finance for development in the rural areas will be declined. Whatever surpluses and wealth the country generates will be transferred to the foreign countries through the multinational companies.

The new economic policy is not a right step in the right direction. The country will lose the economic independence and sovereignty of the new economic policy. The independent economic policy should include the concept of self-reliance, mobilizing internal resources, creating the expanded domestic market by improving the purchasing power of the poorer sections; minimizing the imports, particularly restricting them to the capital good industry; exporting only those commodities which are really surplus after meeting the needs of the people, curbing consumption, unearthing the slack money; progressive taxation, to take loans from IMF and World Bank; according priorities to agriculture and cottage and rural industries; creating infrastructure facilities, taking up massive employment-generation programs including self-employment etc[8].

Public Distribution System (PDS)

The Public distribution system is an important delivery channel in the Management of the food security system in India with a network of 4.35 lakh fair price shops, distributing annually commodities worth more than Rs. 15000 crores to more than 16 crores house holds (16,45,76,000), PDS is one of the largest of its kind in the world.

The basic objective of PDS is to ensure that essential articles are made available to the people at reasonable prices. The nation is committed to reduce hunger and malnutrition. Increase in food production is essential to achieve these objectives. But increased production alone is not enough. Food distribution and consumption are also very critical aspects. Government policies have a major impact on all these dimensions.

The PDS has been an integral part of India's overall food policy. It has been instrumental in mitigating the plight of the masses that are burdened by low income, inflationary conditions, scarcities and the launting fear of adulteration. Intervention by the Government in food distribution started during Second World War and large urban complexes like Bombay and Calcutta were placed under statutory rationing. This has been broad objective of the Government of India since Independence though the nature and relative extent of governmental intervention have been largely conditioned by fluctuations in agricultural production and price rise. It has been foremost in the minds of the food policy-makers that the interest of the vulnerable sections of society must be taken care of in the supply of food grains and essential commodities. The fact is, PDS has been covering all sections of urban and rural people irrespective of income.

The starting point of the government intervention by statutory rationing was during Second World War against the background of the Bengal Famine (1943) era of shortages aimed to benefit government employees and others, which has crucial to sustain war efforts. Later, when the conditions further worsened, the scheme was enlarged to cover the common people. As the war gathered momentum, statutory rationing was enforced and the free market operation was relinquished. Nevertheless, the approach was narrow in nature and designed to meet the exigencies created by the emergent circumstances. It also lacked the backing of sound policy so indispensable to develop this system in the best interest of the consumers.

With the return of normality private traders persuaded the Government to maintain the earlier status quo it yielded to the pressure without going into pros and cons. The consequent decontrol policy resulted in the prompt transformation of suppressed inflation. This charge was mainly caused by inter-alia, artificial scarcities, and into inflation, volatile shifts in agricultural production. Since then from a statutory rationing system, PDS has emerged as a poverty alleviation measure to become a permanent feature in Indian economy. Besides, in the context of new liberal policy it is regarded as a safety net for the poor[9].

The First Plan emphasized the distribution of food grains through the statutory rationing system in cities/ towns above 50000 population and also in highly deficit areas and for other areas a non-statutory ration system was introduced. During the Second Plan the coverage of PDS was extended from food grains to other essential commodities. The third five-year plan placed the importance on public procurement and distribution system for price stabilization. The approach was to introduce institutional changes in the private trade mechanism by including consumer co-operatives.

In the Fourth Plan the scope of PDS was further widened. This system was extended to all the rural areas and other goods of mass consumption were also distributed with the help of co-operative stores. In the Fifth plan, PDS was focused on the poor and it was related to prices, income and wage policy. The Sixth Plan emphasized public distribution of food grains to the disadvantages groups. During the Seventh Plan it was included, as an item of the minimum needs programme. During the Eight plan, emphasis was on intensification of PDS in rural/disadvantaged areas covering several mass consumption articles like salt, pulses, Soap, tea etc., in addition to the six mandatory commodities (i.e., rice, wheat, sugar, edible oil, kerosene and soft coke) and developing infrastructure in terms of creation of new fair price shops and godowns.

The Ninth Five-Year Plan has taken by a broader view of food security to include nutritional security. It categorically states that food and nutrition security is one of the main objectives. It calls for long-term measures for eradication of hunger and starvation of ensuring availability, accessibility and affordability of balanced food and nutrition for all.

The food policy and public distribution in the last five decades, show that barring two spells of decontrol a brief one in 1947-48 and a long one from 1954 to 1956-57 some sort of food control was prevalent. As observed in a domestic set up, a government is responsible to the people in a situation of overall shortage of food and fluctuation in agricultural production. The distribution could not be left to the private trade and free market mechanism on ideological grounds[10].

Statement of the Problem

The New Economic Policy (NEP) being implemented since mid-1991 has progressively started posting new challenges in all the sectors of the economy and is also opening up new opportunities in the national and international markets. Macro Economic Structural Reforms Programme had envisaged deregulation of industries and trade, reduction of the role of public sector and privatisation of financial institutions. This policy has both positive and negative impact on rural poor.

The NEP of liberalization and General Agreement on Tariff and Trade (GATT) agreement have brought about sea change in policy focus. Now, price, trade and distribution will be based on market principle. This perfect liberalised market has only an immediate adverse impact on agriculture by way of sharp increase in input prices and consequently on cost of products. The rise in cost has come at a time when Indian agriculture expects to take up the challenge of globalised market and to provide food security and employment for the growing of the economy. It was further compounded by the reduction of subsidies on fertilizer, electricity, irrigation, credit and public distribution.

The Economic survey 1996 shows that almost 19 percent of India's population live below the poverty line. On August 15, 1996, Prime Minister declared that the PDS would cover only the poorest of the poor, that is, the population living below the Poverty line. This group would be supplied food grains at 50 percent of the central issue price, the price at which, ration shops sell their stock.

The Government's main concern now is to identify the consumer groups on which the PDS should be targeted. In states like Tamil Nadu and Kerala, PDS user accounts for about 10 percent of the state's population. It is difficult for the central Government to impose its policy on the states. The policy of selective and PDS creates situation in its implementation. It is therefore the right time to study the operational aspects of the new policy and to come up with pragmatic strategies for its success. The present study attempts to analyse the impact of economic reforms on Public Distribution system in Tamil Nadu State.

Objectives of the Study

Over all objective of the study is to evaluate PDS in Tamil Nadu during the liberalization era. The specific objectives of the study are:

(i) To find out the rate of reduction in subsidies for supplies through PDS and its effect on PDS prices;

(ii) To analyse the impact of the price and quantity changes of PDS commodities on pattern of total expenditure, consumption, savings of the PDS beneficiaries; and

(ii) To make a comparative study of PDS prices and the open market prices for the commodities distributed under PDS so as to estimate implicit subsidy borne* by the society;

* While the difference between issue price and PDS price in the measure of direct subsidy paid by the Government, the difference between open subsidy, market retail price and the price paid by the PDS beneficiary for the same commodity is the implicit incurred by the society.

Hypothesis

Based on the above objectives, the following hypothesis are framed:

(i) There is positive relationship between the increase of PDS price and the prices of the commodities in open market.

(ii) Given these increases in prices the household's response will be to reduce consumption of commodities (especially those not available in PDS); to put in more efforts to increase their income so as to keep the real income constant.

(iii) While subsidies are burden on the exchequer they have a social benefit in reducing poverty

in terms of calories in take by the poor. In other words subsidies add to the purchasing power of the really needy person in the society and thus improve social welfare.

Concepts

A clear definition of the concepts used in this study of Public Distribution System would help any reader to understand the different issues dealt with the present study. Hence before proceeding with the actual discussion and analysis, an attempt is made to define the various concepts used in the present study.

Beneficiary

Beneficiary as per the Government norms, those who are having ration cards are called beneficiary of PDS. In our study we mean the beneficiary as "who is having ration card and the person receiving or purchasing commodities from ration shops with their own cards or by using the other person's cards".

Non-Beneficiary

Non-Beneficiary, in our study includes not only non-card holders but also the persons do not get any commodity from the ration shop, though they are having ration cards.

Essential Commodities

The Government supplying the basic necessary items of rice, wheat, sugar, rava, maida, kerosene and palmoelin oil are also considered as essential commodities.

Issue price

Issue price refers to the price fixed by the central Government for the essential commodities supplied through PDS. It includes the procurement cost, transport and storage cost and rate of interest, etc.

Procurement

Procurement is done through direct purchase centres opened at village level. In addition to minimum support price fixed by the Government of India, State Government also order to pay incidental charges/incentives to benefit the farmers.

Stock

The Government of India purchase and store the essential food items for supplying to consumer through the Food Corporation of India (FCI).

Allotment

Every month, the Government of India allots necessary food items to the state Government from central pool for eventual distribution through Public Distribution System.

Off-take

On the one hand, the off-take refers to the quantity of commodities for PDS by the State Government from the total allocation of Central Government and on the other hand, it means the utilization of essential PDS commodities from the total allocation of PDS commodities to each district.

Scales of issue

The Government for the supply under PDS to the card holders determines the quantities of essential commodities. This is called as scale of issues.

Methodology

The primary data as well as secondary data were used for the present study. In order to analyze the functioning and performance of PDS in India and Tamil Nadu, data for 10 years from 1986-87 to 1995-96 were collected from the Department of Civil Supplies Chennai. The Budget allocation, subsidy rate, expenditure for PDS, price variation, quantities supplied etc. were analysed with the help of secondary data. For collection of secondary data various sources were tapped. The predominant among them were Directorate of Food and Civil Supplies, Government of Tamil Nadu, Ministry of Food, Government of India, Economic and Statistical Adviser to the Government of India, Krishi Bhavan, New Delhi, Ministry of Finance, New Delhi and District Food and Civil Supplies Controller, Dindigul. In addition to it, officials of Food and Civil Supply Department were also contacted from time to time for clarification and verification of data and for ascertaining their views on the subject.

Data on production, procurement and distribution of wheat and rice were taken from various issues of Bulletin of Food statistics. The data on various subsidies were collected from the Indian Economic Statistics. Secondary data were gathered from population Census of Tamil Nadu, Manual of Nutrition, Co-operative Sugar and Agricultural statistics in India.

For the micro level analysis, Dindigul District is purposively selected for the study because the researcher is familiar with the District. One taluk from the district was selected on the basis of the largest number of PDS Beneficiaries. After selecting sample taluk for the study, one town and one Panchayat in the taluk were selected on the basis of the same criterion.

A sample of 75 PDS beneficiaries and 75 non-beneficiaries of PDS from the sample town and sample block was randomly selected with the help of verifying ration cards. Those families with annual income below Rs. 10,000 are considered as poor and those having income above Rs. 10000 are considered as non-poor, since, Government of Tamil Nadu introduced the changes in the price and quantity supplied under PDS at the mean average annual income of Rs. 10000. A total of 150 PDS beneficiaries and 150 non-PDS beneficiaries were interviewed with the pretested questionnaire. The primary data on various aspects were collected during the year 1999-2000.

A discussion was made with the ration dealers in order to identify the problems faced by the implementers in the effective implementation of PDS in Tamil Nadu. The additional interviews were made with purposefully selected persons namely. Private rice and wheat merchants, government officials known for their commitment, local politicians, representative from traders organizations, etc.

The respondent's response to each of the question in the schedule was first tabulated in master table. The qualitative data were quantified as discussed and tabulated to draw meaningful inferences. Thereafter, appropriate tables were prepared keeping in view the specific objectives of the study of analysing the data with the application of statistical tools.

Simple average and tabular analysis were used to analyse the data. The collected data were analysed with the suitable statistical techniques. Before and after technique and comparative analysis were used to study the impact of the economic reforms of PDS in Tamil Nadu. The reference year was 1993-94 because, in the year Government of Tamil Nadu introduced changes in the PDS in response to the economic reforms.

Importance of the Study

Reducing poverty in India is one of the major development challenges faced in the world. The Government of India has experimented with a number of direct anti-poverty programmes. Of these, the Public Distribution System (PDS) a quantity rationing-cum-food subsidy program-is perhaps the adopt. It has evolved in its present form in the wake of national-level food shortages of the 1960's. Since then, the national agricultural scene has vastly changed to the better, contributing to a substantial fall in the incidence of poverty. However, the PDS remained fundamentally unaltered, and the cost of food subsidy has grown enormously since mid-1980. Moreover, some State Governments have introduced food subsidy programs with additional resources of their own.

Since 1990, India has introduced a wide range of economic reforms, including significant liberalisation. Within these changes towards better regional targeting are being considered. However few studies have estimated the impact on poor household of PDS, in terms of reduction in the incidence and severity of poverty as well as nutrition improvements. The costs per unit of welfare gains have been estimated, in view of the important role-played by safety net programs, both during normal times and the periods of major economic reform. It is hoped that this case study for India would be of interest of researchers and policy-makers engaged in poverty reduction.

Introduced in response to very critical food shortages in mid 1960's, PDS has evolved into a price support-cum-subsidy program. The program has continued more or less unchanged although the food scenario at the micro (state) level has changed from one of scarcity to a surplus situation. PDS subsidies account for substantial budgetary expenditures at the central level. Public spending levels are exceptionally high in states that have their own subsidy programs. Moreover, the country is implementing an economic reform program. At no time is the question of the efficacy of PDS as a safety net more relevant than now, especially since the Government has recently embarked on a drastic reform of the system. Although PDS is an over researched subject in India, few studies have estimated the welfare gains and costs per rupee of income transferred. Almost no studies exist that compare the benefits and costs of PDS relative to other similar programs.

Quantity rationing of essential commodities has been in existence in India since the inter war period. The Public Distribution System (PDS) in its present form a price support-cum-consumer subsidy program - has evolved in the wake of critical, national- level food shortages at the 1960's. The program has probably contributed to a containment of upward pressure on food prices and ensured access of the food to urban consumers. Although the national agricultural scene has vastly changed for the better, contributing to a fall in the incidence of poverty, the food subsidy cost has doubled over the past two decades, and accounted for 0.7 percent of GDP in 1993-94. PDS is now "perceived" to the main safety net to protect the poor from potential short-run, price induced adverse effects on the economic reforms currently under way, but the perception appears to be far from reality.

Not with standing the added emphasis given to PDS in the wake of economic reforms, few studies have estimated the welfare gains in terms of income as well as nutritional impact. Nor have the cost per unit of income or nutritional gains been estimated. It estimates the gains and cost of PDS and compares it with other similar programs. The impact of PDS on the incidence and severity of poverty is also estimated based on the countries own experience and experience of other countries, the Research considers various policy option for reform.

PDS plays an important role in alleviating the problems of the rural poor. More than 80 percent of the people are availing the service of the PDS. After implementation of the New Economic policy in India, PDS are redesigned as revamped PDS and at present targeted only at the poorest of the poor. This approach has the double advantage of helping the really needy while reducing the cost of subsidy to the Government. However, the scheme has to meet with several operational hurdles as those who had enjoyed the benefit for a quite long a time would not easily give up. These studies highlighted such problems and help the administrative of PDS.

Profile of the Study Area

The profile of the Dindigul District and the sample blocks - Dindigul Block, Attoor Block and Dindigul Town are explained in this chapter. The profile includes the location, demography, literacy, agriculture, climate, rivers, administrative divisions, industry, trade, transport, communication, Physiography, forest, livestock's etc.

Dindigul District

LOCATION

Erode, Coimbatore, Karur and Trichy Districts bound the District on the north, by Sivagangai, Karur and Trichy Districts on the East, by Madurai and Theni District on the South and by Coimbatore District and Kerala State on the West. It is spread over an area of 4217.36 sq.km.

ADMINISTRATIVE SET-UP

For the administrative convenience, the Dindigul District is divided into three Revenue Divisions, namely, Dindigul, Palani and Kodaikanal. The district comprised seven taluks. They are Dindigul, Natham, Nillakottai, Palani, Vedasandur, Kodaikanal and Oddanchatram. There are 3 municipalities in the district. They are, Dindigul, Palani and Kodaikanal. The 14 Blocks of the district are: Attoor, Batlagundu, Dindigul, Gujiliamparai, Kodaikanal, Natham, Nillakottai, Oddanchatram, Palani, Reddiarchattram, Shanarpatti, Thoppampatti, Vadamadurai and Vedasandur Block. The district also comprises of 39 Revenue Firkas and 357 Revenue villages.

POPULATION

According to 1991 census, the total population of the District is 17,60,601, which covers the male population of 8,90,783 and female population of 8,69,818.

The taluk wise population is:

Dindigul	: 6,41,378	Natham	: 1,19,222
Nillakottai	: 2,27,976	Kodaikanal	: 3,34,388
Vedasandur	: 2,56,232	Palani	: 98,598
Oddanchatram	: 23,578		

Physiography

The district has extensively hilly and rocky areas with undulating plains. Palani hills forming northern part of the Western Ghats ranging in height from 1000 to 2700 mts. The upper plains with an average height of 2500 mts. comprise valleys and contain several peaks like Perumal Hill, the Vandarvey Hills etc. They consist largely of plateaus made up of rolling down covered with coarse grasses and isolated shoals in the valleys. The lower plains consist of confused jungle of peaks from 1000 to 1700 Mts. heights, separated from one another by steep and beautiful wooded valleys. Those hills are Thandigudi, Virupatchi Hills etc. On the eastern side, Sirumalai, Alagar Malai and the Natham and Ayyalur hills are found. A large number of isolated peaks namely Karumalai, a sacred hill, tapering Kodarangimalai, great rock of Dindigul, Rengamalai etc., are also found. The rest of the District characterised by an undulating plain covered mostly by Red Soil (85%). The upper plains have thick layer of black earth over yellow clay.

River and Irrigation

The river system is complicated to some extent due to several Hills and Valleys and is seasonal dependent on rainfall. The pattern of drainage may be described as dentatric on the plains and sub-parallel to the Hills. The plains around Dindigul and Palani drained north-eastern by four almost parallel tributaries of Amaravathi River rising in the plains. The Vedasandur taluk is drained by Kodaganar and part of Nillakottai taluk by Manjalar. A number of streams flowing in the District mostly drain into tanks.

Semi-arid tropical monsoon type of climate is prevailing in the plains. However upper plains record low temperature and fairly heavy rainfall. In the plains, the Maximum and Minimum atmospheric temperature are 40°C and in the Hill stations 37°C and 8.5°C respectively. Heat becomes intense in April and May and shoots further up unless interfered by rains. There are 41 Government canals, 2612 tanks and 79275 wells in the district. About 29 percent of the net area are irrigated. Wells form the chief source of irrigation followed by tanks. There are 79275 wells to provide irrigation to 68236 ha. Palar-Porandalar, Kodaganar and Manjalar Schemes are important irrigation schemes. Canals irrigate 12310 ha. 2612 Tanks irrigation covers 16607 ha.

Forest

Forest covers 18.8 percent of the total area of the district. Forests fall naturally under 3 main formations, the mixed deciduous the evergreen and the grass land. The natural vegetation is rich and varied. About 700 species accounting for 50 to 80 percent of the flora of whole Indian Peninsulla have been identified in plains besides a large number of species peculiar to themselves.

Agriculture and Land Use

The total geographical area of the District is 508016 ha. Net cultivable area is 274707 ha. Out of the net area sown as low as 9 percent is sown more than once. Dry farming is predominant in the District and the important wetland track is located in the Shanmuganathi and Kodaganar basin. Paddy is the principal crop (37%) followed by oil seeds (23%) fruits and vegetables (24%). Cholam is the major irrigated crop (30%) followed by oil seeds (18%) and paddy (11%).

Sirumalai and Virupathci Hills are known for a special variety of plantains. Fruits like Orange, Lime,

Mango and Grapes are of special interest in Dindigul, Nilakottai, and Palani taluks. Colecrops and temperature fruits growth chiefly in Kodaikanal lower plain. About 900 ha. is put under Kuruvai system of cultivation and the crops raised are Potato, Cabbage, Tenai, Samai, Brinjal, Cotton and Ragi in the forest reserves.

INFRASTRUCTURE

The District has two Universities, Viz, Gandhigram Rural Institute at Gandhigram and Mother Teresa Women University at Kodaikanal. The Nation's prestigious Highway NH-7, passes through the District besides NH-45, and a network of roads. Dindigul is an important Railway Junction. A broad gauge Railway line from Karur to Kanniyakumari has been completed. The nearest aerodrome is located at Madurai, which is 65 kms away.

Marketing facilities are inadequate. Madurai market committee has gained momentum in this direction. Exports of the district include hides, skins and leather, dyes and tans, cotton and silk fabrics, tea, cardigan etc. In 1997, there are 78 post and Telegraphs, 437 Post offices and 3 telegraphic offices in the District. The district has 141 Commercial Bank Branches, 83 Rural Bank Branches, 30 Semi urban and 28 Urban Bank Branches.

INDUSTRIES

Next to farming a sizeable population depends on Industries. Dindigul is the important industrial centre. A number of Spinning Mills are functioning at Vedasandur and Vadamadurai blocks, besides a few paper mills in Swaminathapuram. Tobacco and cigar manufacturing, metal industry, dyeing, iron industry, cotton spinning and weaving are the promising industries.

This districts is having a thriving handloom industry at Chinnalapatti which is located 11 kms away from Dindigul. Chinnalapatti silk sarees and sungadi sarees are famous through out India; More than 1000 families are engaged in these industries. At present, there are 8009 registered small-scale industries and 61 Large and Medium scale Industrial units in Dindigul District.

TOURIST ATTRACTIONS

This District is privileged to have one of the six celebrated hills of Lord Muruga at Palani Hills. Famous Dhandayuthapani temple is situated on the hills. The pilgrims are praying this holy temple during festival days. The important among them are "Sura Samharam"; "Vaikasi Visakam", and monthly karthigais. A provision of three electric winches, the first of its kind in India is a unique feature of this temple. This facilitates the aged, children and disabled to reach the temple by 8 minutes. The income of the temple, which is the large in the state, is growing year by year and now it exceeds Rs. 4 Crores.

Besides this renowned Murugan temple, there is also another Murugan temple at Thirumalaikeni, 25 kms away from Dindigul Town, which is growing into a pilgrim centre. Abirami Amman Temple in Dindigul Town and Rajakaliamman temple at Thethupatti 20 kms away from Dindigul is the other temple worth mentioning. Kodaikanal, popular summer holiday cum health resort, located at an altitude of 2133 meters in the Western Ghats is the famous hill station of this District[11]

Dindigul Block

In the Dindigul block total population including institutional and houseless population are 120030 lakhs.

In particular the Scheduled castes are 32495 and Scheduled tribes are 1813. Total main workers are 58498 and Non-workers are 63981. Number of cultivators are 10111 and net cultivated area is 69 percent of the total area. Number of Agricultural labourers is 23560 in the Dindigul Block.

The Block covers an area of about 32237 hectares. In this block, the total Panchayats are 14, namely, 1. Adiyanoothu, 2. Nalakrishnapuram, 3. Anaipatti, 4. Chettinayakkanpatti, 5.M.M. Kovilor, 6. Kurumpapatti, 7. Mullipati, 8. Pallapatti, 9. Periyakottai, 10. Seelapati, 11. Sirumalai, 12. Thamaraipadi, 13. Thottanuthu and 14. A. Vellodu.

Dindigul Town

It serves as the District Head Quarters of this District, has a holy past. Once this City was under the way of famous king 'Thippu sultan'. This ancient city has a historical Rock Fort, which was constructed by the famous Naik Kinng. Muthukrishnappa Naicker'. Since the shape of the rock resembles cushion, this city is called "Dindigul". It is located between 10.05 and 10.9 North latitude and 77 and 78.20 East longitude.

Dindigul Town Municipality has 45 wards. The Dindigul town's total population according 1991 census is 1,82,293. Total male members are 92750 and female members are 89,543. Total number of household were 43256 in Dindigul Town. The town literacy rate is 63 percent. During the period of Kamaraj, drinking water scheme was provided through the construction of Kamarajar Dam which is 13 km away from Dindigul.

In Dindigul there are 234 commission mandies for selling agricultural products like onion, chillies, groundnut, cotton etc. About 3500 people are working in the tanneries around the town. In addition to manual work shops many timber shops and sawmills are also functioning in this town. For a long time Dindigul Town is associated with locks of good quality and durability. A lock-manufacturing unit under Co-operative sector is functioning here. Another Industry for which Dindigul is noted is leather tanning. The widely known Anguvilas Scented tobacco and Roja supari are produced in this town, and being sent to other places.

Dindigul, which is an important wholesale market for onion and groundnut, has the network of inter-district roads connecting Coimbatore, Erode, Karur, Trichy, Madurai and Sivagangai Districts. Educationally, Dindigul is a well-developed and popular city. It has got many High Schools and Higher Secondary Schools, Colleges and Professional Colleges to its credit.[12]

Attoor Block

Attoor Block is located in the southern region of the Dindigul District. Its northern boundary is the Reddiarchatram and the western boundary is Kodaikanal Block. Batlagundu Block and Nilakottai Block are the southern boundary and Nilakottai and Dindigul Block are eastern boundary of the Attoor Block. Attoor block has a total area of 94.89 sq. Kms. the numbers of occupied residential houses are 31765 and number of households is 31774.

Total population including institutional and houseless population is 136049. In particular, the male population is 68218 and female population is 67831. The Scheduled castes are 29270 and among them male are 14774 and females are 14496. Scheduled tribes population is 266 consisting of males 130 and female 136. In this Attoor block, the total literates are 71337. Among the literates, male are 42841 and females are 28496. In this Attoor block total main workers are 64354. Among the main workers males are 39976 and Females are 24378. There are more number of male cultivators i.e., 17196 male and 7182 female cultivators in the block. The agricultural labourers are totally 34528. Among the total farm labourers, male agricultural labourers are 17910 and female agricultural labourers are 16618.

The block is having manufacturing, processing, servicing and repairs, and other household industries workers. Out of the total 2589 non-farm workers, 1442 are male and 1147 are females. Marginal workers are 2030 including 139 males and 1891 female workers. Non workers population is also very high i.e., 69665 in the Attoor block. In particular, male in non-workers group is 28103 and female is 41562. In this block, Panchayats are 1. Attoor, 2. Akkaraipatti, 3. Alamarathupatti, 4. Ambathurai, 5. Aiyankottai, 6. Podikkamanvadi, 7. Settiyapatti, 8. Devarappanpatti, 9. Gandhigram, 10. Seeval Saragu, 11. Kaligampatti, 12. Manloor, 13. Munnilaikottai, 14. N. Panjampatti, 15. Paraipatti, 16. Palayamkottai, 17. Pillayanatham, 18. Pittalaipatti, 19. Thoppampatti, 20. Vakkampatti and 21. Veerakkal.[13]

The above explained brief profile of the Dindigul District and sample study blocks and town would be very useful in analysing the performance and functioning of Public Distribution System during the liberalisation period.

Review of Literature

The present section reviews a few earlier studies related to the Economic Reforms and Public Distribution

System. The chapter is divided into two parts. The first part reviews the past studies on the Public Distribution System and Food security. The second part reviews some of the studies related to the Economic Reforms and the Public Distribution System.

PUBLIC DISTRIBUTION SYSTEM AND FOOD SECURITY

Dadgostar[14] made a study to provide a method for bridging a large gap, which exist between the theory of consumer demand and estimation of Demand equation, and to apply the methodology to deriving the demand for food commodities at a retail price in Thailand. This study was conducted to improve the understanding of the behaviour of demand for food in Thailand and also to furnish the policy maker with some wastes on Demand structure, which would be useful in development of the agricultural sectors. The result indicating that the total food consumption, which represents fifty percent of the total consumers's expenditure, is not very responsive in the aggregated food price income and aggregate non-food prices.

Srinivasan and Shikkajha[15] found that the Indian government has traditionally maintained buffer stocks as a means to stabilise domestic food grains prices. In the scenario of liberalised external trade in food grains, the study examines the cost effectiveness at variable levies on trade as an alternative option to stabilise domestic prices. The use of variable levies is much more effective in stabilising prices and reducing food insecurity under free trade as compared to the case of no trade.

A study of Suryanarayana[16] revealed that the Indian government is considering food stamp program as an alternative to the public distribution system in order to reduce the budget deficit with least social cost. This study evaluates the experience of such a program in the U.S., Srilanka, Zambia and Jamaica and concludes that the lack of proper socio-economic data on the Indian populance, it would be wise to confine the program to urban locales.

Jos Mooij[17] conducted field survey in two Indian states, Karnataka and Bihar and the study analyses the difficulties of TPDS. In particular, it focuses on some misconceptions and wrong assumptions underlying the introduction of the targeted PDS. Politicians and policy-makers have over looked vested interest and institutional constraints, which often make it impossible or at least very difficult to implement the policies as they were meant to be implemented. He argues that policy discussions are insufficiently grounded. In the day-to-day political and bureaucratic realities at the state and local level, and that this is in part, related to the institutional organisation of the policy making process itself.

Another study examines the volume of the food subsidy over the last three decades, using data for the 1990's from the accounts of the Food Corporation of India (FCI) and the components of the food grain subsidy. The relative contribution of different components to total costs, and relative contribution of different components during the current decades. Thirdly, to compare the efficiency of the FCI with that of private Trade. Finally, no unambiguous finding emerged from a compression of whole sale market prices and economic costs of the FCI. The FCI compared favourably with private traders in the distribution of rice in a large number of states. In the states of northern and central India, however, private traders had lower prices for grain. The presence of systematic rural-urban price differences indicated the imperfections of grain markets[18].

A study of Ravi and Ravi[19] revealed that PDS alone will not solve the problem of food security. Apart from higher economic growth, a mix of policies such as effective implementation of anti-poverty programmes including PDS is also needed. Ambiga Devi[20] reveals that the government policies has been significant in attaining self-sufficiency in food grains production, in supporting producers through procurement prices and subsidies and in distributing essential food item through PDS. The number of persons below the poverty line or the per capita calorie intake on the budgetary resources. One could realise that the government has to still go a long way to announce proudly that it has given "Food Security to all in India". Uma Sankar[21] suggested that the New Panchayat Raj system could solve the problem of food security in the rural areas to a greater extent.

Ahmed[22] estimated that low-income urban consumers consumed 250 calories more per person due to subsidised rationing system in Bangladesh. Kumar[23] analysed the impact of food price subsidy on level of food consumption and nutrition of a low-income population in Kerala, India. The study found that for all the measures of household dietary quality and nutrition, the amount of ration subsidy had a significantly positive impact and there was a 35 percent net calorie increment from ration calories. Edirsinghe and Navellie[24] estimated that the food subsidy scheme contributed 151 calories per person in the lowest expenditure quintile, which constituted eleven percent of the total calorie intake by the expenditure group. This contribution was merely 0.6 percent in the highest expenditure quintile.

Ajit Kumar Ghose[25] pointed out that the famines are caused not generally by absolute food shortages but by sudden increases in inequality of food distribution. Such changes are most often brought about by a decline in food production and sometimes by a rise in the relative price of food. The severity of effects of food depends on the structural characteristics of the rural economy concerned, the pattern of land distribution. The proportion of population depends on exchange for acquiring food supplies. These are also variables whose temporal movements are control to the long-term process of generation of poverty and inequality. The links between famines and long-term impoverishment do not end here. A famine, by accounting the inequality in the distribution of productive assets among rural households, contributes to the longterm process of generation of poverty and inequality.

Ragbendrajha[26] analysed the policy allocation of food grains, the Public Distribution System by using four sets of pooled equation for predicting stable levels of per capita consumption of rice and wheat in physical terms in rural and urban India. Food grain demand is estimated for all states. A formula that is based on the concept of subsiding real consumption through PDS is proposed.

Madura Swaminathan[27] conducted a study on revamping Public Distribution System in Maharashtra. The study conducted at household level in Goreagan Village of Maharashtra the 42 household could not afford to buy the common variety of rice in the market either. And the study explained that they purchased broken rice at a rate of Rs. six to seven per kilo through irregular supplies of grains through the Revamped Public Distribution System, and consumer paid more in the private market than in the fair price shop and they did so far a commodity of lower quality.

Mahendra Dev[28] found that there are no major initiatives in the Budget to arrest the disturbing trends in agriculture, rural development and poverty. In the case of the Public Distribution System (PDS), the government is following poor strategies and these are reflected in the budget. Some strategies are needed for agricultural development and for improving the effectiveness of the RPDS in the light of the budget proposals.

Another study of Mahendra Dev[29] examined the poverty and food security problem in Maharashtra and West Bengal. The study also argues through the wider reach of the PDS makes it more effective they the Employment Guarantee Schemes (EGS). Further, proper targeting and improved delivery system in rural areas will make the PDS more efficient. Nevertheless, not PDS alone, but a mix of policies involving effective implementation of anti-poverty programmes, controlling inflation, improving facilities, will be needed to solve the food security problem in India.

Grover[30] in his book highlights the very useful and pertinent information with regard to the identification of the beneficiaries and Cost-Benefit analysis of PDS. The analysis of the impact of the Public Distribution System on food grains prices and projection of food grains and sugar requirements for Public Distribution System under the different normative situations generates revealing findings useful for policy purpose. The study also states that keeping in view the twin objectives of economic development with social justice the food subsidy may be continued in the near future. However, it may be restricted to the vulnerable population only.

Raja Purohit[31] suggested that in rural areas all those who were not operating land might be regarded as vulnerable. Thus, the vulnerable sections in the rural areas belonged to the non-land operating; mainly consisting of land-less labour, artisans, etc. In the urban areas, it was found that as per NSS 28th round (1973-74), nearly 25 per cent of the urban population in Karnataka consumed cereals less than State average consumption for the urban areas. Such sections might be properly identified on the basis of the income of the household and may be issued ration cards. On this criterion, the study estimated the target group population both for urban and rural areas for the year 1971. In total, there were 6.3 million persons in the State of Karnataka who were really vulnerable and needed help. About 1.8 million and 4.5 million persons of such group belonged to urban and rural areas, respectively.

Singh[32] remarked that the essential condition for the success War that should not be leakage that can allow the movement at commodity from controlled markets to the free Markets. The study shows that the controlled scarce commodity had easy access to black market and control shops keep sign board always displaying stock position as Nil. He suggested that the system could work well only when there was a vigilant and organised consumer interest and honest, efficient and effective administrative machinery.

George[33] estimated that the impact of discontinuation of food subsidy on nutritional status in the states of Kerala and Gujarat. He calculated that in Kerala, calorie intake went down by 46 per person amongst the higher income group and by 138 amongst the lowest income group. The highest loss of 244 calories per person, however, was to the household of the low middle income group (Rs. 1201-2400 annual household income). For Gujarat, the loss was estimated to 192 calories and 178 calories per person to the house hold of lowest income group and highest income group respectively.

Kabra[34] revealed that PDS segment of food market was very thin in its spread and found that per capita annual off-take from PDS to the total consumption level of the poorest strata comes out to be only 1/6th or 1/5th. The study suggested three propositions concerning future policy for PDS:

(i) The relative share of the PDS in total food supply should be increased to such an extent it is able to influence the behaviour of the open market segment.

(ii) Direct availability of a larger share of the PDS to the poor: both in urban and rural areas would serve the objectives of PDS.

(iii) Opening more retail outlets without increasing the total off-take and supplies under PDS may be counter-productive.

Bapna[35] reported that India was among one of the countries of the world which had too less of calories available on per capita basis (2189 calories) whereas world average and Asian average was found to be 2666 and 2437 calories, respectively. As per the study of Erenson, the estimates of the poor in India in 1982-83 were as high as 57 percent and reported that considering an average requirement of 2550 calories; the proportion of undernourished population in urban and rural areas was 66.12 percent and 51.73 percent respectively.

Indrakanta[36] analysed the working of PDS in Andhra Pradesh. The study highlighted the structural changes in it and with the help of Simulation exercises, some of the important issues concerning government intervention policies were examined. For the examination of policy-effects, the year 1985-86 was taken as the reference year. The study concluded that the rice welfare scheme transfer welfare from the rich to the poor. It was not having the marked impact on producer. For Government, it implied a heavy expenditure on subsidy. In 1985-86, it was estimated that a supply of 2.15M. Tonnes through PDS involved a subsidy of Rs. 2097 million (Central and State). Thus, subsidy per tonne worked out was Rs. 975.

Nair[37] concluded that an ideal public distribution system should be responsive, socially oriented, public participation and cost effective. He further stressed that the services should be made available closer to doorsteps through increasing the selling points. It is reported that there were about 3.41 lakh retail units of PDS in the country and private individuals ran majorities of them. Out of this, 2.70 lakh retail unit were located in the rural areas. Nation-wise data shows that the country had only one fair price shop within a radius of 9 sq.mt.

Upadhyay[38] considering fact that the poorer segments of our society are ill-equipped to face and absorb the shocks of liberalisation policies, not withstanding many economic, political and administrative factors which prevent the full realisation of its potential; the PDS is highly relevant scheme, which needs to be further strengthened. There is a general consensus among economists that to make it more effective in providing food security to the poor, the PDS should be linked with poverty alleviation and employment guarantee programme and the price of food grains sold through the PDS should be drastically curtailed. A country flush with huge stocks of food grains can hardly have any justification for wide spread malnutrition and semi-starvation.

Madi[39] in his article has analysed the existing system of distribution in India; and also discussed various concepts of operation and measures for the effective functioning of the system. Lal Sahab Singh[40] in his article has analysed various problems of the public distribution system in India with a view to giving a new direction.

Singh[41] examined the effectiveness of fair price shops in fulfilling the twin objectives of food relief and price stability. It dealt with the viability of fair price shops, the buying patterns of ration card holders and the extent of benefits available from fair price shops to the consumers, their difficulties with fair price shops and the like. On the basis of this study suggestions were offered for reforming the fair price shop system. Sankaraiah and Sundarshan[42] made a study at Warangal and found that the Public Distribution System is based as a device for making private profit by means and consumers are helpless even to assert the drawing of their monthly ration from fair price shops. This study too lacked rural courage. Pulapre Balakrishanan[43] explores the idea that the decline of Foodgrain production in Kerala originated in the decline of agriculture following migration to the Gulf and points out the implications of the consequent import dependence of food supply in the state.

ECONOMIC REFORMS AND PUBLIC DISTRIBUTION SYSTEM

Praduman Kumar and Mathur[44] have analysed that the household income and food prices strongly influence the pattern of food consumption. However, rapid structural transformation may have an important influence on food demand in the long run. Many pervious studies have ignored the possible influence of structural shifts on food demand. The study examines the changes in the consumption pattern and decomposes the changes in consumption pattern due to the price, income and non-price factors.

According to Thamarajakshi[45] the state intervention in the food grain market has to be considered in the light of the over all objectives of structural adjustment and economic liberalisation as also the impressive trends in cereal production. Public distribution of food grain should be directed only for securing food to the poor at low prices. For the purpose targeting PDS should be area specific and group specific. Allocation for welfare scheme such as the mid-day meal scheme and for payment of wages in kind to labourers in rural employment schemes should continue.

Kailash and et al[46] conducted a study on the effect of subsidy on household consumption in Western Tamil Nadu. Studies on food consumption provide ample evidence that atleast 30 percent of the population is either undernourished or malnourished, indeed a staggering magnitude. In Tamil Nadu, the Public Distribution System of food and non-food and the free meal scheme are the two major programmes covering the entire population, comprising children and old under its fold. The study concludes that the noon meal scheme plays a pivotal role to help enhance the enrolment of rural and urban low-income group children in Primary schools besides improving their health and status.

Shahnawaz Malik[47] reviewed that the targeted food subsidy is a short-term measure for rural poverty alleviation in Pakistan. The present exercise considered four food items, viz. wheat, rice, coarse grains and pulses. The desegregated expenditure elasticities by income stratum suggest that the latter two food items seem highly likely to be suitable for an effective self-targeting. This is because the ratio between low-income and high-income elasticities is considerably higher as compared to earlier two food items. More over, the high-income elasticities give extremely low values which helps further targeted subsidies.

Soundarapandian[48] concluded that after implementation of economic reforms, the highest percentages of the poor are purchasing the food grains from the open market. But the highest percentages of the rich are getting food grains from PDS. The percentage share is unequal distribution. Further, the recent announcement of covering the whole country under PDS is a welcome change, but it is too early to assess how it will help the rural poor, if there is no change in the operational mechanism.

Mahendra Dev[49] noted that PDS is not only the answer to food security of the poor because it can help only those who have purchasing power. Apart from higher economic growth, a mix of policies like effective implementation of anti-poverty programmes, stabilisation of prices, improving wealth facilities is needed for raising food security at the household level.

Another study of Madura Swaminathan[50] found that in many countries reduction in food subsidy has occurred as part of programmes of structural adjustment and had adversely affected consumption and nutrition. In India, too consumer food subsidies have fallen since 1991. The reduction in forced subsidies has come about, despite little change in the budgetary allocation to food subsidy by means of sharp price increases for commodities sold in Fair Price Shops by a fall in quantities supplies to the system of public distribution, and by a reduction entitlements in certain cases. In a period of low growth and high inflation, the public distribution system failed to ensure that the prices of major food staples were low and stable.

George[51] suggested the following points: (1) restrict the volume handled through PDS by means of effective targeting and reduced leakages. (2) Match the procurement, both in terms of commodity composition and volume, with distribution target so that storage levels' can be controlled; (3) increase the efficiency of handling operations, especially the operation of Food Corporation of India.

Jha[52] pointed out that the Indian Public Distribution System, which was one of the largest of its kind in the world, was inefficient and needed to be overhauled. The study pointed out that ration shops were better accessible, in urban than in rural area in all the States and Union Territories. The main contributory factor to this difference turned to be the distance from the ration shops, while crowding seems to be similar in both rural and urban areas. The study highlighted that since it was not possible to clearly separate out the tastes and preferences of the targeted from non-targeted population, the idea of self-targeting did not click. Therefore, a PDS needs reorientation for a more effective targeting.

Suryanarayana[53] observed that in 1985-86 food subsidy accounted for Rs. 1891 crores of which Rs. 1373 crores was consumer subsidy and Rs. 518 crores was for buffer stock operations. It was further observed that PDS met less than 20 percent of the purchases of the poor for the majority of the commodities (except sugar, kerosene). These percentages were similar for all income groups. The study concluded that the PDS marginally supplemented and did not really protect the vulnerable sections of society. It is suggested that the PDS supplied should be targeted i.e., limited only to vulnerable sections of society and their PDS entitlement may be enlarged.

Jos Mooij[54] concerns with a system, which even after seventy years of inceptions, continuous to remain an issue in public debate and policy in India. In recent years, this system has increasingly been criticised for being costly, and ineffective. On the other hand, the PDS is also presented as an absolutely necessary social-safety net to help the needy during difficult periods of time. Something, which acquires additional importance in the context of the several economic policies, introduced since 1991. Further, he had adopted a broad perspective on the public distribution system and explores how it works reality who protest, who is excluded and why this is the case.

Radhakrishnan and Subba Rao[55] had reviewed that the PDS subsidies account for substantial budgetary expenditure of the central level and public spending level are exceptionally high in states which have their own subsidy programs. Moreover, the country is implementing an economic reform programs, At no time is the question of the efficacy of PDS as a safety net more relevant than now, especially since the Government has recently embarked in a drastic reform of the system. This paper finds out the recent development with respect to prices and off-take are then assessed in the light of the past performance of the PDS, current developments and international experience. Of all poverty-targeted programmes, PDS rice scheme appears to be the least efficient in terms of transfer gains and costs.

Mahendra Dev[56] found that the increase in rural poverty level in the post-reform period was more due to the direct and indirect impact of reforms as compared to factors. One of the main factors could be the inability of the states and the centre to undertake relief works in order to increase the purchasing power of the rural poor. Thamarajakshi[57] reviews that efficiency considerations prevail in public spending in agriculture and market signals are allowed to come into full play so that changes in agricultural investment and production prices. Government should focus on productive investment; technology and research, marketing and storage and agro-processing facilities and provision of food safety nets for the vulnerable poor development of a diversified agricultural in line with emerging demand patterns.

Suresh D. Thendulkar and et al[58] reviewed impact of the economic reforms since July 1991 on poverty. This study provides the available evidence from the National Sample Surveys conducted during 1991 (July-December) and 1992 (January-December). Contrary to prior expectations, there was a sharp increase in rural poverty whereas only a moderate rise took place in urban poverty. Based on the analysis of the factors governing rural and urban poverty and the supplementary empirical evidence, the study concluded that the economic reforms related decisions contributed indirectly rather than being the only or the major cause of the sharp acceleration at rural poverty during the period under consideration.

Gupta[59] attempted to study the impact of the economic reform measures on the poor by looking at (i) the effect of these measures on income and consumption in agriculture and the informal small industry sector. (ii) The performance of safety net programme to protect the new poor exposed the adverse impact of reform in the short run. (iii) The direct and indirect effect of the government social services and human development programmes in the pre-and post-reform periods and (iv) the employment picture of the country in the post-reform period. The results of the study are mixed, but in general they showed the social costs of reforms. While they may have been low as compared to those in many other developing countries, are nevertheless high enough to demand a corrective course.

A study of Martin Ravallion[60] focused that there are understandable concerns about the effects on India's poor of higher food prices stemming from recent or proposed policy reforms. Over 24 rounds of the National Sample Survey, spanning 1959-94, one find a strong positive correlation between the relative price of food and India's poverty rate. This article questions how reform critics have interpreted this correlation. It is not an income-distribution effect. Rather it appears to be due to covariant fluctuations between average consumption and food prices due to other variables, including food supply during bad agricultural year's simultaneous lower rural living standards and increased food prices. The correlation is uninformative about the welfare effect of a sustained increase in the relative price of food.

Suryanaryana[61] suggested for the PDS reform based on commodity orientation system largely from the general impression that (i) the commodity basket of the PDS is weighted in favour of commodity which figure prominently in the budgets of the middle and rich income groups, and (iii) coarse cereals are consumed largely by the poor and hence an approach to ensure targeting would be changed the commodity composition of the PDS in favour of coarse food grains. This study examines the empirical bases for the suggestion for reform by reorienting the PDS commodity composition.

Raj Kapila and Uma Kapila[62] made study on Prices and Public Distribution System in Agricultural Policy. They concluded that the inherent strength of the economy to compact inflation and bring about price stability in the near future lies in its stable food economy, high industrial growth potential, fairly good performance of infrastructure sectors, improvements in foreign exchange reserves, expectations of positive impact of structural reforms and liberalisation policies on the over all productivity and growth of the economy, and above all the strong will and firm determination of the Government to remove the Macro-economic imbalances, both internal and external.

Baskar Majumber[63] reviewed the Public Intervention in Indian agriculture in connection with food scarcity historically since the Bengal famine of 1943 and the food scarcity during the Second World War. He concentrates in this paper on the implication of liberalisation of Indian agriculture in the domain of public procurement and distribution of food grains and food security. The existence of a highly skewed distribution of land holdings, the division of the producers between group with low and high marketable surplus, the division of the consumer's between rich and poor, the non-institutional character of rural market, the dominance of the traders in rural product market etc. indicates the rational of government intervention in Indian agriculture. The required task is to guide it in the context of liberalised thought to ensure the efficiency of such intervention. This lies in targeting the small and marginal farmers on a priority basis while selecting the producers-cum-sellers of food grains, inclusion of those slum dwellers in urban areas and landless labourers in rural areas as probable buyers from the fair price shops and exclusion of the non-poor from this network of Public Distribution.

Krishna Rao[64] viewed that the implementation of the second generation of economic reforms needs to be approached cautiously in the present state of the world economy. The current phase of globalisation may hold potential for economics with high levels of competitiveness based on high productivity and highly skilled labour force. Evidence from several countries has shown that market reforms imposed on economics at low levels of social sector development like-literacy skills, nutrition and health-are not likely to yield expected results. Infact, reforms without "safety nets" through social sector expenditure and ensuring food security through the PDS.

The reviews of past studies related to the Economic Reforms and Public Distribution System could pave the way for analysing the impact of economic reforms on the Public Distribution System in Tamil Nadu.

REFERENCES

1. R.P. Singh, *"New Economic Policy and Perspective to Rural Development,"* National Institute of Rural Development, Hyderabad, 1997.

2. *The Economist*, September-20, 1997.

3. Y.V. Krishnan, *"Indian Agriculture in the contex of Globalisation"*, Proceeding of the Seminar on Rural Prosperity and Agricultural Strategies and Policies for the next millennium, NIRD, Hyderabad. 1999.

4. Amit Bhaduri, *"Economic Structure of Backward Agriculture"*, Macmillan Publication, Delhi, 1983.

5. Krishnasamy. K.S., *"Agricultural Development Under the Economic Regime"*, Economic and Political Weekly", June-25, 1994.

6. Vyas V.S. *"New Economic Policy and Vulnerable Sections Rationale for Public Interventions"*. Economic and Political Weekly, March 6, 1993.

7. Joshi S.S. *"New Economic Policy, Institutions for Agricultural Sectors,"* Ist Annual Conference of AERU, held at IARI, NEW Delhi. 1993.

8. Utsa Patnaik, *"Towadrs A Recolonisation of Indian Agriculture"* Paper Presented at three-day seminar on New Economic Policy" held at Hyderabad, 1993.

9. Jos Mooij, *"Food Policy and the Indian State.* The Public Distribution in India",. Oxford University Press, New Delhi, 1999.

10. A.C. Jena, *"PDS an over view of Policies and Programme Implementation"*, R.C. Choudry & S. Rey's Kutty (ed), Fifty Year of Rural Development in India retrospect and Retrospect," NIRD, Hyderabad, July, 1998.

11. Assistant Directorate of Statistics. Dindigul District collectorate, Dindigul. 2000.

12. Municipality Office, Dindigul. 2000.

13. Office Records About Panchayat Union Office. Sempatti. 2000.

14. B Dadgostar, *"Integrated approach to demand analysis for food in Thailand"*, Economic Affairs, Vol.22, Quart 3, September, 1997.

15. P.V. Srinivasan, Shikhajha, *"Food Security through price stabilisation: Buffer stocks Vs variable levies"*, Economic and Political Weekly, Vol. XXXIV, Nos. 46 & 47, November 20,1999, pp. 3299-3304.

16. M.H. Suryanayana,*" Some Experiments with Food Stamps"*, Economic and Political Weekly, Vol. XXX, No: 52, December 30, 1998 pp. A 151-159.

17. Jos Mooij. *"Dilemmas in food policy about institutional contradictions and vested interests"*. Economic and Political Weekly, Vol. XXXXIV, No: 52, December 25, 1999 pp. A 120-144.

18. Madura Saminathan, *"Understanding the costs of the Food Corporation of India"* Economic and Political Weekly, Vol. XXXIV, No. 52, 1999. pp. 121-32.

19. G. Ravi and A. Ravi *"Food Security and PDS in India"* Peninsular Economist, Vol. XI, No. 1, 1998-99.

20. P. Ambiga Devei, *"Food Security and Government Intervention"* Peninsular Economist, Vol. XI, No: 1, 1998-99.

21. G. Uma Sankar, *"New Panchayat Raj System an Agenda for food security in India"*, Peninsular Economist, Vol. XI, No. 1, 1998-99.

22. R. Ahmed, *"Foodgrain supply, distribution and consumption policies within a dual pricing mechanism. A case study of Bangladesh"*, Research Report No. 8. International Food Policy Research Institute, Washington, D.C. 1979.

23. Kumar, Shubh. K, *"Impact of subsidised rice of food consumption and Nutrition in Kerala"*, Research Report,

No. 5, International Food Policy Research Institute, Washington, D.C. 1979.

24. Edirisinghe and Neveille, *"The Food stamp scheme in Sri Lanka Costs, benefits and options for modification"* Research Report No. 58, International Food Policy Research Institute, Washington, D.C. 1987.

25. Ajit Kumar Ghost, *"Food supply and starvation* A study *of famine with reference to the Indian sub-Continent"* Oxford Economic Papers, Vol. 34, No: 2, July, 1982. pp. 369-89.

26. Raghbendra Jha, K.V. Bhanu Murthy and et al, *"Real consumption levels and Public Distribution System in India"*, Economic and Political weekly, Vol. XXXIV, April, 10-16, 1999, pp. 919-28.

27. Mudura Swaminathan, *"Revamped Public Distribution System a field report from Maharashtra."* Economic and Political weekly, Vol. XXX No. 36, September 9,1995. pp. 2230.

28. S. Mahendra Dev, *"Agricultural Development and PDS: lack of major Initiatives"*, Economic and Political Weekly, Vol. XXXV, No. 15, March 25, 2000 pp. 1046-49.

29. S. Mahendra Dev, *"Food Security a PDS Vs EGS. A Tale of two State"* Economic and Political Weekly, Vol. XXXI, No. 27, July 6, 1996, pp. 1752-1764.

30. R.K Grover, *"Public Distribution System: A Socio-Economic Analysis"*, Classical Publishing Company, New Delhi 1998.

31. Rajapurohit A.R. *"Economic analysis of procurement and public distribution of food grains in Karnataka"*, Indian Journal of Agricultural Economics, Vol. XXXIV, No. 3, 1979.

32. P.N. Singh, *"Supply Management Through Public Distribution System"* Glimpses of Planning and Economic Policies in India, Capital Printing Service, Delhi.

33. P.S. George, *"Public Distribution System in Kerala Income Distribution Implications and Effectiveness"* Research Report No.7, International Food Policy Research Institute, Washington, D.C. 1979.

34. Kabra, Kaman Nayar, *"On the inadequate size, urban bias and universal coverage of public distribution system"* Quarterly Economic Report, The Indian Institute of Public Opinion, Vol. XXXII, No. 4, 1989.

35. Bapna S.L. *"Food Security through the PDS: The Indian Experience"* In Tyagi D.S. and S. Vyas (1990), Increasing access to food; The Asian Expense, Sage Publications, New Delhi, 1990.

36. Indrakanth. S. *"Public Distribution System in Andhra Pradesh with special reference to rice"*, Indian Journal of Economics, Vol. LXXII, No. 3, 1992.

37. Nair, T.G. *"Strengthening of PDS"* The Financial Express, September-9 1992.

38. V. Upadhyay, *"Inflation, Food Security and Public Distribution System,"* Social Action, Vol. 6, No. 3, July-September 1996.

39. K.R. Madi, *"Public Distribution System in India"*, Southern Economist, July-11, 1991, pp. 17-18.

40. Lal Sahab Singh, *"Public Distribution System in India with special Reference to food grains"* Southern Economist, June-15, 1982, pp. 17-18.

41. Singh V.B. *"Evolution of Fair Price Shops"*. Oxford and IBH Publishing Company, New Delhi, 1973.

42. Sankaraiah and Sundarshan, *"Empirical assessment of Public Distribution System"*, Indian Journal of Marketing, Vol. No. 5 January 1984.

43. Pulapre Balakrishnan, *"Land Reforms and the question of food in Kerala,* "Economic and Political Weekly, Vol. XXXIV, No. 21, May 22-28, 1999 pp. 1272-80.

44. Praduman Kumar and V.C Mathur, *"Structural changes in the demand for food in India,* "Indian Journal of Agricultural Economics, Vol. 51, No. 4. October-December 1996.

45. R. Thamarajakshi, *"Economic Reforms and State intervention of foodgrain market"*. Economic and Political weekly, Vol. XXXII, No. 30, July 26, August 1, 1997, pp. 1894-1900.

46. A.C. Kailsh C. Suyambulingam and C. Sekar. *"A study on the effect of subsidy on household food consumption in western Tamil Nadu,"* Artha Vijana, Vol. 35, No. 2 June 1993. pp. 150-59.

47. Shahnawaz Malik. *"Targeted food subsidy as a short-term measure for rural poverty alleviation in Pakistan"*, Economic Affairs, Vol. 38, Quart 1, March 1993. pp. 57-60.

48. M. Soundarapandian. *"Food security in the context of New Economic Reforms"* Peninsular Economist, Vol. XI, No. 1, 1998-99.

49. S. Mahendra Dev, *"Public Distribution System: Impact on poor and Options for Reform"* Economic and Political Weekly, Vol. XXXI, No. 27, July 6, 1996, pp. 1752-1764.

50. Madura Swaminathan, *"Structural Adjustment, Food Security and system of Public Distribution of food,"* Economic and Political Weekly, Vol. XXXI, No. 26, June 29, 1996 pp. 1965-1967.

51. P.S. George *"Public Distribution System food subsidy and production incentives"* Economic and Political Weekly, Vol. XXXI, No. 39, September 28, 1996, pp. A-140.

52. Jha Shikha. *"Targeting Subsidies: what needs to be done?"* Monthly Public Opinion Surveys, Vol. XXXVII, No. 1, 1991.

53. M.H. Suryanarayana, *"Revamping of PDS"*, Financial Express. August 22, 1991.

54. Jos Mooij. *"Food policy and the Indian state: The Public Distribution System in South Indian"* Oxford University Press, Calcutta, 1999.

55. R. Radha Krishna. K. Subbarao, and et al. *"India's Public Distribution System, A National and International Perspective"* World Bank Discussion Paper No. 380 Washington 1999.

56. Mahcndra Dev," *Economic Reforms and the Rural poor"*, Economic and Political Weekly, Vol. XXXIV, No. 21, May 22-28, 1999, pp. 1272-80.

57. R. Thamarajakshi, *"Agricultural And Economic Reforms"* Economic and Political Weekly, Vol. XXXIV, No: 33, August 14, 1999, pp. 2293-95.

58. Suresh. D. Thendulkar. L.R. Jain. *"Economic Reform and Poverty"*, Economic and Political Weekly, Vol. XXI. No. 23. June 10, 1995, pp. 1373-77.

59. S.P. Gupta, *"Economic Reform and its Impact of Poor"* Economic and Political Weekly, Vol. XXX, No. 22, June 3, 1999 pp. 1295-1312.

60. Martin Ravallion, *"Reform, Food prices and Poverty in India"*, Economic and Political Weekly, Vol. XXXIII, No. 1&2, January 10, 1998. pp. 29-39.

61. M.H. Suryanarayana, *"PDS reforms and scope for commodity* based targeting", Economic and Political Weekly, Vol. XXX, No. 13, April 2, 1995. pp. 687-95.

62. Raj Kapila and Uma Kapila," *Understanding India's Economic Reforms"*, Vol. IV, Academic foundation Delhi. 1996.

63. Basker Majumber," *Liberalisation of Indian Agriculture Implications for the Home Market for Food grains"* Proceeding of the seminar on Rural Prosperity and Agricultural strategies and policies for the Next Millennium, November 4 & 5, NIRD Hyderabad. 1999.

64. Y.V. Krishna Rao, *"Indian Agriculture in the Context of Globalisation"* Proceeding of the seminar on Rural Prosperity and agriculture strategies and policies for the Next Millennium, November 4-5, NIRD, Hyderabad, 1999.

2

Public Distribution System: *A Performance Analysis*

The present chapter has been divided into two parts. The first part analyses the origin and growth performance of public distribution system in India. The functioning of Public Distribution System in Tamil Nadu is explained in the second part of the chapter. The growth performance analysis deals with procurement, stock, distribution, prices and subsidy etc.

Public Distribution System in India

Origin

The Public Distribution system in India forms an important part of state strategy for intervening in the distribution of food grains and other essential commodities. However, the nature of the policy of state intervention is largely determined by the causes and conditions, which are responsible for its emergence and growth. The major causes of the origin of this policy are 1. Drought, famine and war conditions, 2. Inflation, 3. Market imperfections, 4. Poverty and 5. Lack of distributive justice.

The primary impetus for the growth of Public Distribution System in India has been shortage of essential commodities from time to time. These shortages were caused due to war, famine, drought and natural calamities. Thus, the emergence of Public Distribution System in India has been more in response to some specific critical situation rather than to conscious public policy. British Government imposed the Second World War on India. There was popular opposition to the mobilisation of the war efforts. This anti war climate came to be exploited by hoarders and black marketers to serve their basal interests. As war advanced, the prices of food grains steadily rose.

From September 1939 to September 1942, the British Government called six Price Controls conferences. Price control came to be introduced in India in 1941. Controlled distribution of food grains became necessary after the fall of Burma, the most important supplier of rice to India, in March 1942. The importance of linking Price control, with a control on distribution of food grains, was stressed by the fifth price control held in April 1942. The British Government issued the food grains control on May 21, 1942. This order originally covered major food grains (wheat, rice and barley), but subsequently the coverage was extended to pulses and millets as well. From 28th May 1942, the futures and options in wheat and gram were prohibited as anti-speculative measures with the permission the central Government or an authorised office, throughout British India. The attitude of the British Government to the Quit India Movement as well as the Japanese threat further worsened the food situation on December 2, 1942. The Government of India established the Food Department, with a view to integrate all the activities regarding the purchase, distribution and movement of food grains on all basis.[1]

Until 1940, there was an insignificant rise in price. It was after March 1941 that the upward trend of prices started. By 1942, wheat prices have almost doubled and by 1943, the price index had gone up to 387. This period of Indian history was characterised by intermingling of economic and political issues. The arrest of national leaders in the August 1942 Movement created an anti-British, which was fully exploited by the hoarders, black marketers and profiteers. The public felt that the official purchases and exports led to the rising prices. In utterdisregard to the evil of harding, people favoured decontrol and a trial was given to it in January 1943. Contrary to the expectations, the prices soared up immediately after the decontrol. The disastrous free trade policy was soon abandoned in July 1943.

In July 1943, the First Foodgrains Policy Committee, under chairmanship of Dr. Theodore Gregory was appointed and was entrusted with the task of recommending a sound and effective food policy for the subsequent years. Its recommendations emphasised the need for increased supply, improved procurement machinery, execution of rationing, statutory price control, overhauling of the administrative machinery and a closer co-operation between the centre, provinces and princely states.[2] The Foodgrain enquiry committee recommended the need for price stabilisation, control over trade of food grains and its "Progressive Socialisation". The Committee was of the opinion that full control of food grain market was neither desirable nor feasible. Instead, the committee suggested open market purchases of the wholesale trade and regular imports of rice and wheat to meet local consumption requirement.

The recommendations of the committee were implemented only partially. The food imports under PL

480 were used to distribute large quantities of food through fair price shop at prices. In 1959, the Government fixed minimum and maximum levels of open market prices, but it was abandoned within one year. During 1964-65, the Government set-up Agricultural Price Commission and Food Corporation of India. The role of Agricultural Price Commission was to advice the Government on appropriate price policy for agricultural commodities. The Food Corporation of India was to function as an agent for State and Central-Government to handle local procurement, storage, buffer stock operations and inter state movements of food grains. Along with the setting up of these two agencies, the procurement efforts were intensified and rationing was introduced in all the cities with a population of more than 10 lakhs. Since the year 1967-68, the rationing through the fair price shops has begun to be described as 'Public Distribution System", in the Government Policy documents.

A new phase of distribution system emerged in 1969 exactly after 30 years of its beginning. The fourth five-year plan set out the guidelines for public distribution system. The main feature of this scheme was the creation of buffer stock of adequate size to meet the needs of Public Distribution System. During 1970-71 the output of food grains reached what was then a record level of 8.6 million tonnes. Consequently, the instrument of public Distribution system was thrown out of gear. When the food prices started rising at the close of 1971-72 the Food Corporation of India started open market sales for January 1972, inspite of this the prices kept on increasing and by mid 1972, The policy had to be abandoned. Food grains were imported to meet the requirements of Public

Distribution System and the machinery of public distribution system was strengthened. The number of fair price shops increased from 1.21 lakhs in December 1971 to 1.86 lakhs in December 1972. In April, 1973, the wholesale trade in wheat was taken over by the Government of India in order to procure adequate stocks for distribution through Public Distribution System. But the whole sale trade in wheat never got off the ground and it was abandoned in 1974.[3]

Organisational Structure

The organisational set-up of PDS is a mixture of Union and State tasks and responsibilities. The Government of India decides, in dialogue with the relevant States, how much food grain should be procured in each State. It also decides on procurement prices. This is done on the basis of advice from the Commission for Agricultural Cost and Price (CACP), which calculates the cost of production and estimates a reasonable remunerative price for the farmers. In principle these prices are the same for each State. There are different prices for different qualities, but there are no price differentials that relate to ecological and/or other production conditions. In the implementation of procurement policy, individual status makes small adjustment always upwards to these recommended prices.

The FCI has many large warehouses in different parts of the country where food grains are stored after procurements. Food may be transported according to decisions made by the Government of India (GOI) in consultation with state governments. Apart from allocation to the States, the GOI also fixes the issue price

FIGURE 2.1

Farmers and Traders

——Procurement Prices

Food Corporation of India

——(FCI) Issue Prices

PDS Wholesale

—State Food and/or Civil Supplies Corporations

–Co-operatives

–Private PDS wholesale dealers

–FCI (Tamil Nadu)

PDS Retail

in ration shops or Fair Price Shops, run by

–State food and /or civil supplies Corporations

–Co-operatives

–Private PDS retail dealers

——PDS price

Consumers/Card Holders

Source: Department of Food and Civil Supplies, Chennai.2000.

that is selling price of the FCI. As far as distribution within the states is concerned, the state government is, again, the policy-making institution. It can decide how to distribute the allocated food (to everybody to targeted groups only, to concentrate on cities or on rural areas, etc) and at what price.

Each state has its own distribution policy. The state Department of Food and/or Civil Supplies monitors this distribution process. In many states, trading corporation have been established which act as·(PDS) wholesalers. They bring food from FCI warehouse to storage places near to the retail points, the so-called fair price shops. The retail sale of PDS commodities is undertaken either by this state corporation or by co-operative societies or by private fair price shop owners.

This is a schematic outline (Figure 2.1) of flows of foodgrains and distribution of responsibilities. It is important to add that not all procured foodgrain is readily available for distribution. Further more, the above described scheme is (a) cross-cut by several GOI distribution programs meant for selected categories of people in which not the state government but the central Government formulates distribution policy, and (b) supplemented with additional state government programs in the sense of procurement and distribution activities.

It is a schematic outline (Figure 2.2) of the PDS the neglect of the open market in foodgrains. This is a schematic view of the whole foodgrains market in South India. The figure clearly shows a dual market system. The PDS exists alongside the open market. The flow of foodgrains is at the top of the figure. The largest part of the foodgrains is challenged to the open market, while about 10 per cent of rice and wheat goes to the PDS

FIGURE 2.2

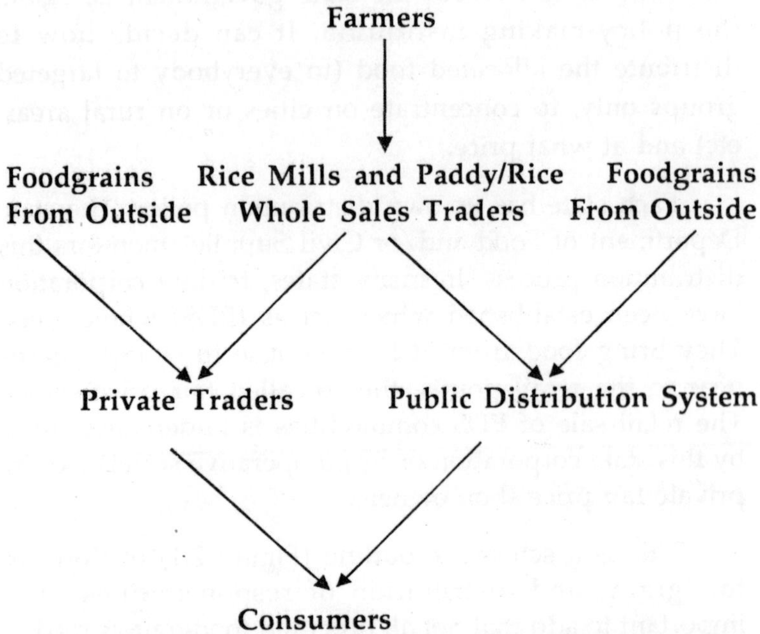

A Schematic view of the Foodgrains Market in South India: Parrallel Markets.

Source: Department of Food and Civil Supplies, Chennai, 2000.

consumer. It focuses on rice production and procurement as there is hardly any wheat production in South India. Both the open market and the PDS are partly supplied by foodgrains stock from outside the State.

The figure of a dual marketing system (Figure 2.3) presents a highly idealised picture. In reality there are many cross-connections. The flow of foodgrains does not just split at the top, only to come together again at the botton when consumers buy from both sources. At many more points within the chain there are exchanges and interconnections.

FIGURE 2.3

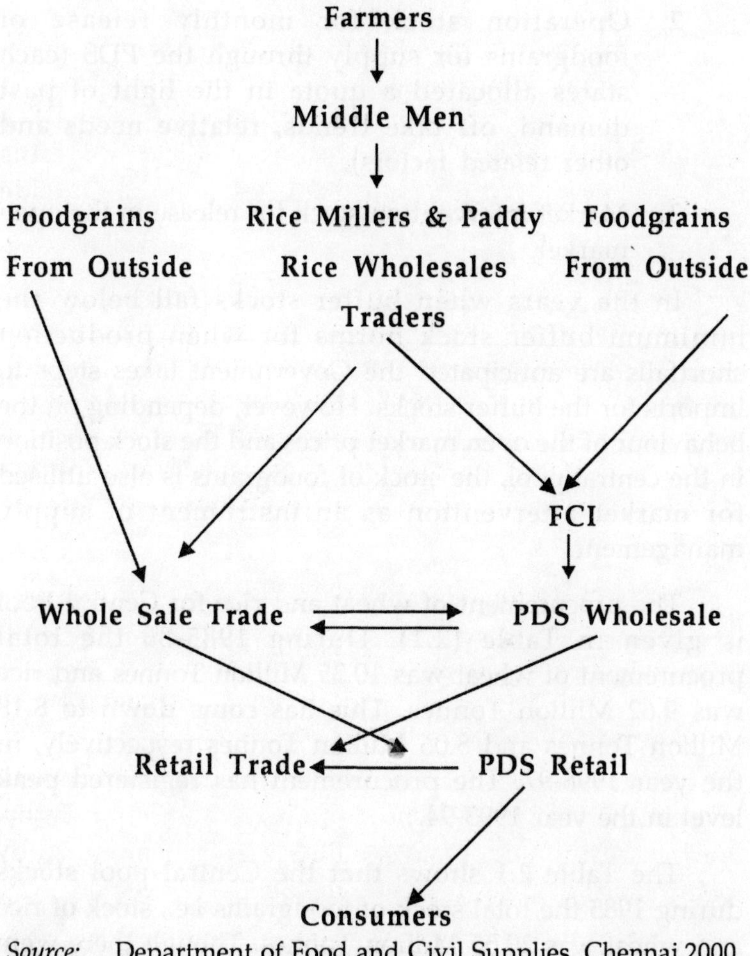

Source: Department of Food and Civil Supplies, Chennai.2000

Procurement, Off-take, Stock of Foodgrains, Issue Prices and RPDS

Procurement of foodgrains is one of the central pillars of the food management policy. The Central government maintains food stocks commensurate with requirements of:

1. The prescribed minimum buffer stock for food security,
2. Operation stock for monthly release of foodgrains for supply through the PDS (each states allocated a quota in the light of past demand, off take trends, relative needs and other related factors),
3. Market intervention stock for release in the open market.

In the years when buffer stocks fall below the minimum buffer stock norms for when production shortfalls are anticipated the Government takes steps to imports for the buffer stocks. However, depending on the behaviour of the open market prices and the stock position in the central pool, the stock of foodgrains is also utilised for market intervention as an instrument of supply management.

The procurement of wheat and rice for Central Pool is given in Table (2.1). During 1985-86 the total procurement of wheat was 10.35 Million Tonnes and rice was 9.62 Million Tonnes. This has come down to 8.18 Million Tonnes and 8.06 Million Tonnes respectively, in the year 1996-97. The procurement has registered peak level in the year 1993-94.

The Table 2.1 shows that the Central pool stocks during 1985 the total stock of foodgrains i.e., stock of rice and wheat was 20.55 Million Tonnes. Though there were lot of fluctuations in the buffer stocks, the actual buffer norms for 1st January of every year is 15.40 Million Tonnes, during the scarcity Government used to import wheat to face the demand.

The annual allocation for wheat has been about 10 million tonnes. The off take of wheat was 8.79 million

Table 2.1

Procurement, Off-take and Stock of Foodgrains

(Million tonnes)

Fiscal year	*Procurement*			*Off-take*			*Stocks*		
	Rice	Wheat	Total	Rice	Wheat	Total	Rice	Wheat	Total
1973-74	3.93	4.5	8.46	3.23	6.90	10.1	2.06	0.91	2.97
1977-78	4.57	5.16	9.73	4.32	7.06	11.38	6.68	8.65	15.33
1981-82	7.02	6.59	13.61	6.74	6.69	13.43	6.36	4.55	10.91
1984-85	9.82	9.30	19.12	6.61	6.72	13.33	8.58	12.47	21.05
1985-86	9.62	10.35	19.97	7.40	11.72	19.12	10.34	10.21	20.55
1986-87	9.36	10.54	19.80	9.03	10.35	19.38	10.04	9.44	19.48
1987-88	7.04	7.88	14.92	10.11	12.78	22.89	5.91	3.34	9.25
1989-90	11.17	9.00	20.17	7.48	7.51	14.99	7.06	3.46	10.52
1990-91	13.02	11.07	24.26	7.87	7.09	14.94	10.21	N.A	N.A
1991-92	10.45	7.75	18.25	10.00	10.48	20.74	8.80	2.21	11.07
1992-93	12.72	6.38	19.00	9.89	8.06	17.95	9.93	2.74	12.67
1993-94	13.6	12.84	26.40	9.46	9.14	18.60	13.55	7.00	20.55
1994-95	13.12	12.33	22.24	14.00	12.44	13.20	25.70	13.24	26.80
1995-96	9.91	11.87	24.99	24.99	8.85	10.59	14.44	19.00	7.76
1996-97	11.87	8.16	20.03	12.44	13.20	25.70	13.17	3.24	16.41
1997-98	14.51	9.30	23.81	11.36	7.76	19.12	13.05	5.08	18.12
1998-99	11.43	12.65	24.08	11.83	8.90	20.73	11.74	9.92	21.96

Source: Ministry of Food and Civil Supplies, Government of India, Report on Currency and Finance, RBI, Economic and Political Weekly, March-18, 2000

tonnes in 1991-92 dropped to 4.83 million tonnes in 1994-95. As for rice, the annual allocation has continuously increased from 11.36 million tonnes in 1992 to 13.32 million tonnes in 1994-95. As against these allocation the annual off take of rice has continuously declined from 9.95 million tonnes in 1991-92 to 8 million tonnes in 1994-95. The increasing procurement and the declining off take have caused stocks of foodgrains at FCI godowns to reach unmanageable levels. The stocks of foodgrains were at 30.1 million tonnes in January 1995 and it reached the peak of 35.6 Million Tonnes in July 1995. The country does not need a buffer stock of more than 15.4 million tonnes of foodgrains in the month of January to tide over and problems caused by unforeseen factors like a monsoon failure. The extra stocks are being maintained at an enormous cost to the nations; the carrying charges of buffer stocks were Rs 1853 crores in 1994-95. Even though the problem of malnutrition and semi-starvation is widespread in the country, the Food stocks at FCI have been increasing primarily because the people's purchasing power has diminished in recent years. Huge FCI stocks give a false impression of abundance.

Table 2.2

Periodic Revisions in PDS Central Issue Price

(per tonnes)

	Rice			*Wheat*	
Date of Revision	*Common*	*Fine*	*Super Fine*	*Date of Revision*	
1990 (June)	289	349	370	1990 (March)	234
1991 (Dec)	377	437	458	1991 (Dec)	280
1993 (Jan)	437	497	518	1993(Jan)	330
1994 (Feb)	537	617	648	1994 (Feb)	402

Source: Economic Survey, 1995-96.

It is not correct to say that sale of foodgrains through the PDS has dropped because people have been switching from the PDS to open market. In fact, the rising issue prices have helped to keep the open market prices above levels that the market would otherwise have determined.

In recent years the difference between the free market and the PDS prices has narrowed down significantly. The poor cannot afford to purchase food in adequate quantities either from the PDS or the open market because prices of food from both the sources have been going up sharply. The real beneficiaries of large increase in procurement prices have been the surplus farmers of wheat and rice in 3 or 4 states which as account for nearly 90 per cent of the procurement. The huge outlays in the name of food subsidy helps sustaining food prices at very high levels. The total subsidy borne by the central government was Rs 5100 crores in 1994-95 and it has been budgeted at Rs. 5250 crores for 1995-96.

In January 1992, the Rao government launched a special scheme. Revamped Public Distribution System (RPDS) which aimed scheme in a more efficient way the tribal, hill and arid area populations located remotely and having a poor infrastructure. This scheme is operating in 1775 blocks. An additional quantity of 3.1 lakh tonnes of foodgrains (rice and wheat) is envisaged to be distributed in these areas. It is RPDS to all the 2446 employment Assurance Scheme (EAS) Blocks. Under this scheme, foodgrains are allocated to states for the proposed to expand the geographical coverage of RPDS blocks at prices lower by 50-paise/kg than the issue price for the normal PDS. The retail price at the RPDS shops is not supposed to be higher than the Central Issue price (CIP) by more than 25 paise/kg. [4] The "leakages" in the system are pointed out as one argument against PDS and it is asked that the same amount invested in the employment generating schemes would yield better results for the poor. These arguments are not tenable. There are "leakages" in the employment schemes also. Besides, for a basic necessity like food a minimum security must be assured to the vulnerable sections. A subsidised PDS for the well-targeted groups is the best form of food security that we have been able to find out. [5] Targeting, however should not just aim at the exclusion of non-needy but should also try to include the needy poor who at present are not covered by the PDS in many states. For states like Kerala and Jammu and Kashmir, the question of PDS reform is essentially a question of targeting the weaker sections of society. But for states like Bihar, MP, Orissa, Rajasthan and UP in particular, the PDS reform should involve substantial enhancement of the quantum of the PDS before targeting and redistribution. [6]

Distribution

The public distribution system is supplied to insulate the consumer from the impact of rising prices of essential commodities and maintain the minimum nutritional status of our population.

Table 2.3

Public Distribution of Foodgrains in India

Year	*Distribution of foodgrains (in Million Tonnes)*	*Year*	*Distribution of foodgrains (in Million Tonnes)*
1960	4.9	1991	20.8
1965	10.1	1992	18.8
1970	8.8	1993	16.4
1975	11.3	1994	14.0
1980	15.0	1995	15.3
1985	15.8	1996	20.5
1986	18.6	1997	20.5
1989	16.4	1999	17.4

Source: Ministry of Food, Directorate of Economic and Statistic, 1999. Department of Agriculture and Co-operation, New Delhi 1996.

The Table 2.3 shows the PDS supplies in India from 1960 to 2000. The foodgrain supply was increased 18.6 million tonnes in 1988 to 20.8 million tonnes in 1991. It is clear that the supply of foodgrains continuously increased and the Government of India was fully involved in the supply of foodgrains to the card holders.

Table 2.4
Public Distribution of Rice and Wheat in India (in M.Ts)

Year	*Rice*	*Wheat*	*Total*	*Percentage of Rice in Total PDS*
1971	3.23	4.46	7.69	42.00
1980	6.06	8.82	14.88	40.73
1981	6.40	6.43	12.83	49.83
1986	8.46	8.50	16.96	49.88
1990	9.03	6.89	15.92	56.72
1991	11.33	9.24	20.55	55.04
1992	10.56	8.43	18.99	55.61
1993	10.46	5.94	16.40	63.78
1994	10.10	6.01	16.11	NA
1995	9.32	5.98	15.30	NA
1996	NA	NA	20.5	NA
1997	NA	NA	20.5	NA

Source: GOI, Directorate of Economics and Statistics, 1994, Economic Survey, 1997-98.

The Table 2.4 shows the distribution of Rice and Wheat in India for the period from 1971 to 1997. In 1971, the supply of rice and wheat was 3.23 and 4.46 million tonnes respectively. The respective figure for the year 1995 was 9.32 and 5.98 million tonnes. But the total supply of foodgrains has been increased from 7.69 M. Tonnes in 1971 to 20.5 M. tonnes in 1997. There were simultaneously increases for the growing population in India.

Table 2.5

Major State-Wise Share of Public Distribution in India (in percentage)

States	Year			
	1979-80	1989-90	1995-96	1999-2000
Andhra Pradesh	6.1	13.5	23.6	23.8
Assam	4.9	4.6	4.8	NA
Karnataka	4.0	6.5	10.3	10.2
Kerala	13.4	16.9	12.8	15.1
Madhya Pradesh	8.9	2.4	2.2	3.9
Maharashtra	8.2	6.5	3.9	NA
Tamilnadu	5.0	17.1	17.3	19.6
Uttar Pradesh	9.3	2.9	2.3	7.0

Source: GOI, Directorate of Economics & Statistics, 2000.

The distribution of foodgrains in major statewise is given in Table 2.5. In 1980, the supply of foodgrains was 13.4 per cent in Kerala and during 1999-2000, the supply of total foodgrains was 23.8 per cent in Andhra Pradesh. Tamil Nadu is the second place of the total supply of foodgrains i.e., 19.6 per cent.

A paradoxical situation has emerged in that both procurement and distribution prices more or less equal to open market prices. PDS off-take has declined, procurement, though, was very high. Consequently the buffer stock has tripled in 3 years right closure more than 37 million tonnes in June 1995, as compared to buffer stock added to the Food Subsidy Bill. In January 1996, the stocks were reduced again to 25 million tonnes, but not because of increasing PDS off-take because of open market sales and exports. [7]

At the central level, there was revamping PDS efforts for the reallocation of PDS foodgrains to 1700 selected blocks, without any formal decision to exclude the other 3400 blocks hence forward. From 1997 onwards, there is a differential pricing system: poor households get PDS foodgrains at a lower price than households not classified as poor. At the level of the individual states, there are similar schemes. This type of targeting can never contribute to a reduction of the system. It only means the PDS expands and becomes more expensive.

Thus what we witness in the 1990s is a Janus-faced policy. On the one hand, issue prices have been increased in an effort to curtail food subsidies and to reduce the system. On the other hand, new expensive schemes are created to serve the poor. Contradictory as it is Janus-faced policy enables the government to pursue various strategies and serve various interests simultaneously. First, the interests of farmers and/or traders who profit from procurement. In the mid-1990s farmers movements are still an important political phenomenon to be reckoned with capitalist agriculturist have formed powerful lobbies and they are represented almost all political parties. No political party can afford to neglect these interests, moreover, with a Prime Minister, from South and increasing representation of Southern interest in the central state. It is no longer mainly the wheat lobby from North India is able to exercise pressure on foodgrain price policy, but increasingly also Southern rice producers. [8]

Economic Cost and Subsidy

Food Subsidy

The central government expenditure on food subsidy increased eight fold in current prices (about two times in real terms) between 1980-81 and 1992-93. The rate of growth of central government expenditure on food subsidy slowed down after 1993-94. However the share of food subsidy of GNP as well as in central government expenditure, has fluctuated showing no strong secular trend one way or another.

In 1994-95, out of the food subsidy amount of Rs. 51000 million, subsidies for cereals and buffer stocks accounted for Rs. 42041 million (about 82 per cent). A notable development is the sharp increase in the annual carrying cost of buffer stocks both absolutely and relative to total food subsidy. It increased nearly three fold over the period from 1990-91 to 1994-95. On the other hand, the expenditure on cereal subsidy has declined by 27 per cent between 1992-93 and 1994-95. The distribution of the cereal subsidy for wheat and rice was more or less equal except in the year 1994-95, when the share of wheat has increased to 65 per cent. The subsidy on coarse cereals has been negligible. [9]

The PDS performance in providing food security to the poor has been far from satisfactory. In the past few years the importance of PDS as on outlet of steep and frequent increase in procurement prices followed by the more than proportionate increase in the central issue prices of foodgrains. 51 and 56 per cent respectively between 1990-91 and 1993-94 raised the procurement prices of common paddy and wheat. At the same time, the central issue prices were raised even more by 85.8

Table 2.6

Central Government Expenditure on Food Subsidy in India

Year	*Expenditure (Rs Million)*		*Expenditure as Percentage*	
	At current Prices	*At 1980-81 Prices*	*GNP*	*Total Government Expenditure*
1979-80	6000	6689	0.58	3.24
1980-81	6500	6500	0.53	2.89
1981-82	7000	6359	0.49	2.76
1982-83	7100	5961	0.45	2.33
1983-84	8350	6466	0.45	2.32
1984-85	11000	7927	0.53	2.51
1985-86	16500	11032	0.71	3.11
1986-87	20000	12511	0.77	3.12
1987-88	20000	11506	0.68	2.84
1988-89	22000	11703	0.63	2.70
1989-90	24760	12172	0.61	2.60
1990-91	24500	10863	0.52	2.33
1991-92	28500	11018	0.53	2.53
1992-93	28000	9903	0.45	2.22
1993-94	55370	17871	0.78	3.80
1994-95	51000	14920	1.61	3.01
1995-96	52500	NA	NA	NA
1996-97	70000	NA	NA	NA
1997-98	79700	NA	NA	NA
1998-99	91000	NA	NA	NA
1999-2000	94350	NA	NA	NA
2000-2001	82100	NA	NA	NA

Source: FCI Performance Budget Documents, Economic Survey, Various Issues, The World Bank Discussion Paper No: 380,1997.

per cent for common rice and 71.8 per cent for wheat between June 1990 and February 1994. This has resulted in a PDS that offers cereals at prices, which are out of reach of poorer households. It is not surprising that the off-take through the PDS has been declined continuously since 1991-92. [10]

It can be seen that the economic cost exceeds the average sales realisation and the difference is being met by the central subsidy. The central subsidy per quintal fluctuated depending upon whether or not the increased in procurement price is passed on to the consumer through a corresponding increasing in issue price. Thus, in 1992-93, wheat subsidy increased by 40 per cent price to the consumer was not raised immediately. In the following years as the issue price was adjusted upwards, the wheat sudsidy rate has declined somewhat, though it continues to be higher than in 1990-91. In general, the increases in procurement prices been passed on the consumers by increasing in issue prices.

For the years 1993-1994 purchase cost and distribution costs do not add exactly up to economic cost due to adjustment for stock prior costs etc. Net procurement price represents the prices paid for Wheat and rice procurement cost include (i) mandi charges made up of market fee, auction fee rural development, commission to Kutcha Archaliyas (ii) payments to mandi labour (iii) forward charges (iv) internal movement charges (v) cost of gunny used in bagging the grains (vi) Purchase tax (vii) Charges paid to state agencies for establishment storage and interest. Distribution costs include cost incurred on transportation, interest, storage, grain losses, handling labour, administration over heads, charges paid to state agencies for procurement and stocks held by them till taken over by FCI.

Table 2.7

Details of Economic Cost and Subsidy For Distribution Operation in India

(Rs. Per quintal)

Items	Wheat					
	1990-91	*91-92*	*92-93*	*93-94*	*94-95*	*95-96*
A. Average Net Procurement Price	204.68	211.20	295.51	325.21	334.80	351.10
B. Procurement Cost	64.34	87.69	89.28	89.28	110.86	109.28
C. Total Purchase Cost(A+B)	268.02	298.89	384.79	414.49	454.34	460.38
D. Distribution Cost	87.48	91.90	120.02	117.44	105.51	103.19
E. Economic Cost	365.50	390.79	504.10	532.03	551.17	563.57
F. Sales Realisation	239.95	251.68	279.96	355.88	407.89	415.87
G. Subsidy	116.85	139.11	224.74	176.15	143.28	147.20
H. Sales (M.Ts)	8.89	10.29	8.05	9.15	10.59	13.50
I. Subsidy Amount (Rs. Million)	10365	15006	18096	16112	15178	19940

Source: Performance Budget of FCI, The World Bank, 1997

Table 2.7 A

Items	Rice					
	1990-91	*91-92*	*92-93*	*93-94*	*94-95*	*95-96*
A. Average Net Procurement Price	338.42	572.45	433.73	500.40	537.77	584.60
B. Procurement Cost	41.46	32.69	31.53	40.25	58.13	52.98
C. Total Purchase Cost (A+B)	379.88	405.14	465.25	540.65	595.90	637.58
D. Distribution Cost	87.48	91.96	120.02	124.45	98.31	109.14
E. Economic Cost	457.52	497.04	585.27	665.10	694.71	746.72
F. Sales Realisation	330.02	365.58	442.40	500.42	600.75	610.70
G. Subsidy	127.50	131.46	142.87	164.68	93.96	136.02
H. Sales (M.Ts)	8.12	10.58	9.90	9.49	8.86	12.80
I. Subsidy Amount (Rs. Million)	10352	13903	14141	15626	8329	17410

Source: Performance Budget of FCI, The World Bank, 1997

Public Distribution System in Tamil Nadu

THE ORGANIZATION STRUCTURE OF PDS IN TAMIL NADU

The organization structure of PDS in Tamil Nadu is given in chart No. 2.4 and working of PDS is given in chart No. 2.5. It is found that there are two wings functioning under the control of Registrar of co-operative societies. One wing concentrates on Chennai district only and the rest for other districts. At the Circle level a separate Deputy Registrar (PDS) is looking after the functioning of PDS. At present there are about 150 lakh cardholders in Tamil Nadu. They receive their essential articles from 20960 Fair Price Shops (FPS) run by co-operatives and 10783 FPS run by Tamil Nadu Civil Supplies Corporation. (TNCSC).

TAMIL NADU CIVIL SUPPLIES CORPORATION LIMITED (TNCSC)

The Tamil Nadu Civil Supplies Corporation Limited, a State Government undertaking was formed as a Private Company Under Companies Act 1956, in 1972. It became a Public Limited Company in 1975. The corporation started with a modest turnover of Rs. 12 crores in 1972-73. It increased steadily and the turnover reached to the tune of Rs. 344.64 crores in 1983-84. The turn over increased to Rs 2802 crores in 1996-97. The Board of Directors comprising senior officers administer the corporation. A Chairman and a Managing Director have been appointed. For administrative convenience and decentralisation, the Corporation has 29 Regions, one for each Revenue District. The Senior Manager/Regional Managers head the Regions. There were 10,500 regular employees on roll as on 1.3.98.

FIGURE 2.4

Public Distribution System Organizational Structure in Tamil Nadu

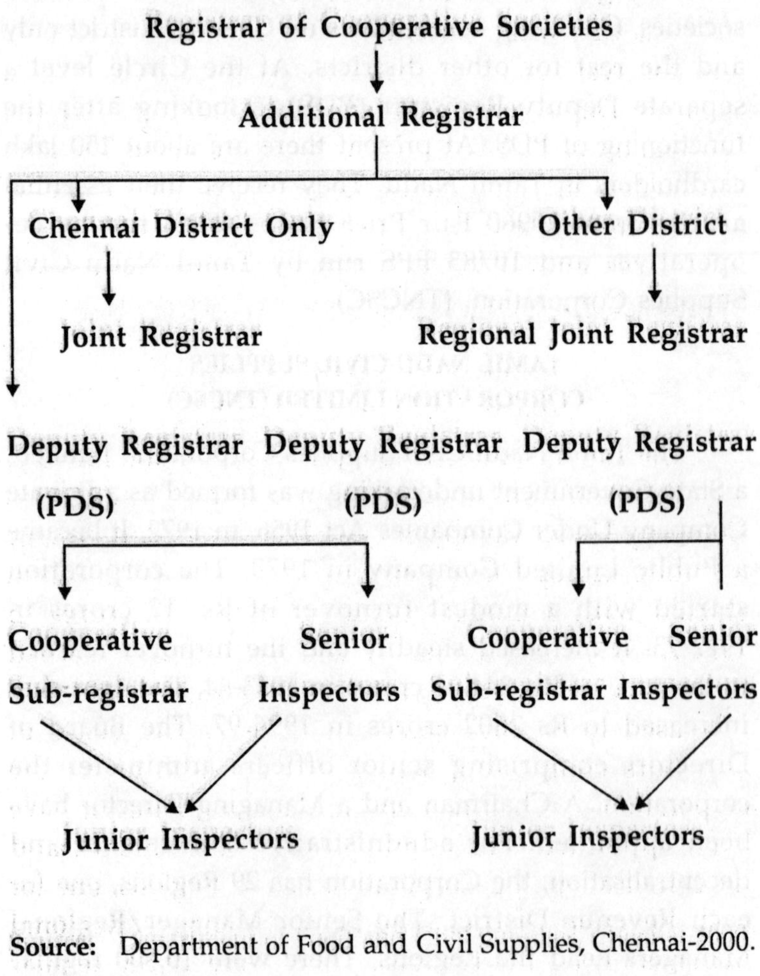

Source: Department of Food and Civil Supplies, Chennai-2000.

FIGURE 2.5

Working of Public Distribution System

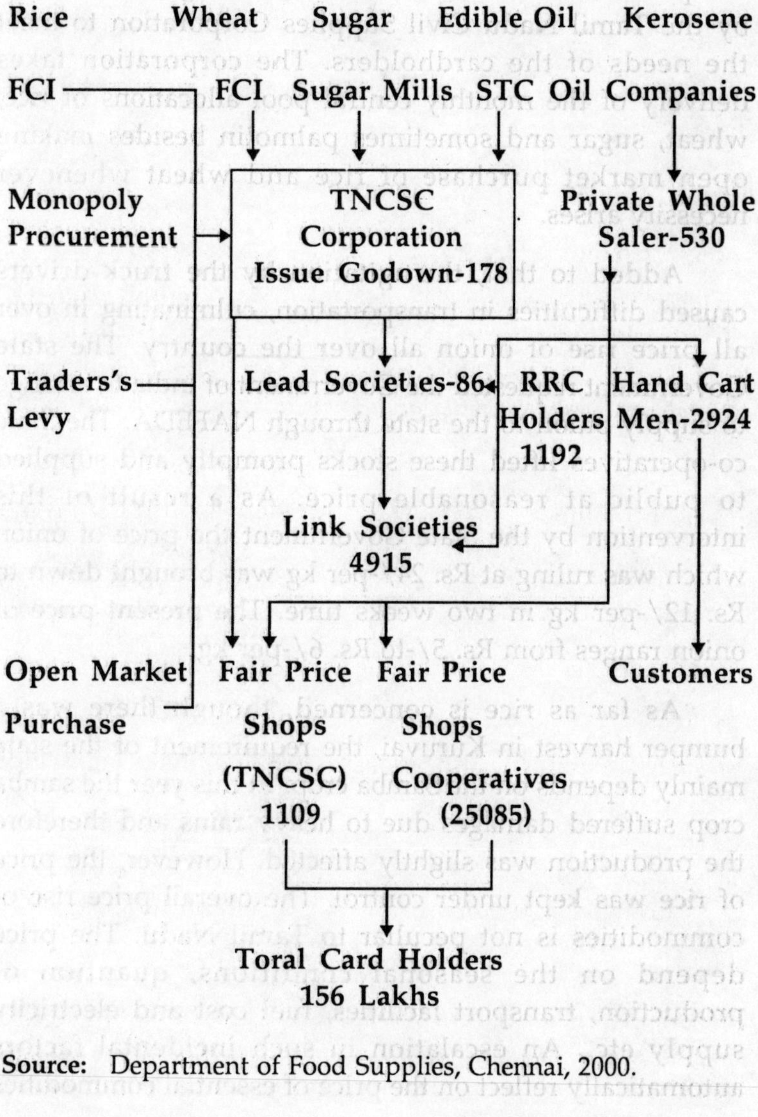

Source: Department of Food Supplies, Chennai, 2000.

The Tamil Nadu Civil Supplies Corporation plays an important role in the field of Public Distribution System, by acting as a wholesale agent of the Government of Tamil Nadu by procuring and distributing all commodities except kerosene. Retail outlets numbering 1110 are run by the Tamil Nadu Civil Supplies Corporation to meet the needs of the cardholders. The corporation takes delivery of the monthly central pool allocations of rice, wheat, sugar and sometimes palmolin besides making open market purchase of rice and wheat whenever necessity arises.

Added to that, the agitation by the truck drivers caused difficulties in transportation, culminating in over all price rise of onion all over the country. The state Government requested the Government of India to arrange to supply onion to the state through NAFEDA. The State co-operatives lifted these stocks promptly and supplied to public at reasonable price. As a result of this intervention by the State Government the price of onion which was ruling at Rs. 24/-per kg was brought down to Rs. 12/-per kg in two weeks time. The present price of onion ranges from Rs. 5/-to Rs. 6/-per kg.

As far as rice is concerned, though there was a bumper harvest in Kuruvai, the requirement of the state mainly depends on the Samba crop. In this year the samba crop suffered damages due to heavy rains and therefore the production was slightly affected. However, the price of rice was kept under control. The overall price rise of commodities is not peculiar to Tamil Nadu. The price depend on the seasonal conditions, quantum of production, transport facilities, fuel cost and electricity supply etc., An escalation in such incidental factors automatically reflect on the price of essential commodities all over the country. Therefore, to control the price of essential commodities the state Government monitors the price situation continuously.

Open Market Price of essential commodities depends on the quantity available in market, level of consumption and the purchasing power of public. The State Government has been constantly contouring the prices of essential commodities in the open market, enabling the Government to intervene in the event of any increase in price. The weekly exports on open market prices of all essential commodities are being received from the District Collectors and registered in the computer system and compile for the state as a whole. Through the computer network, the prices of 139 Essential Commodities are watched and evaluated. The Government has also constituted a committee under the Chairmanship of Chief Secretary consisting of Secretary, Corporation, Food and Consumer Protection, Secretary Finance and Secretary Agricultural of members to monitor the prices of essential commodities on a regular basis. Such monitoring enabled the Government to foresee the unprecedented price rise in respect of onions during the beginning of this year. But this price rise was effectively encountered by the timely market intervention of the Co-operatives as per the orders of the Government. Due to inclement weather the production of onion crops was affected resulting the price rise at the production centres.

The Corporation also supplies commodities to various Welfare schemes such as:

1. P.T.M.G.R. Nutritious Meal Programme Scheme.
2. O.A.P. (Old Age Pension Scheme).
3. Police/Fire/Prison Personnel.

4. Refugees of Sri Lanka.
5. Supply of food grains to Adi-Dravidar/ST and SC/MBC Hostels.

The Corporation supplies essential commodities like rice, sugar, wheat, wheat-products, edible oil to the personnel in police, prison and Fire services up to the rank of Inspector of Police, at 50% of Public Distribution System issue price. The hostels run by Welfare Departments are provided with essential commodities on credit-basis. The Government of India have introduced the scheme of National Programme of Nutritious Support to primary Education (1-5 class) Mid-day meal with effect from 15th of August 95 and this scheme is implemented in the Districts of the State except Chennai. Under this scheme, the Government of India supplies 3 kgs of Rice/Wheat per month per child free of cost. Transport and Handling Charges at Rs. 25/-per quintal are reimbursed to the Tamil Nadu Civil Supplies Corporation by the respective District Rural Development Agencies. The Tamil Nadu Civil Supplies Corporation embarks of market intervention through its Amudham Departmental stores by selling groceries, cosmetics etc. at rates lesser than open market price. At present, 44 the Corporation operates Amudham Departmental Stores in 5 districts. The sale performance of Amudham Departmental Stores up to 12/97 is Rs. 12.05 crores. It is excepted that the sales during the current year will be Rs. 15 crores. [11]

Tamil Nadu Warehousing Corporation (TNWC)

The Tamil Nadu Warehousing Corporation was established in December 1957. The corporation commenced its activities with effect from 02.05.1958 with the main objectives of providing facilities for scientific storage of agricultural produce, seeds, fertilizer, agricultural implements and notified commodities and to help the depositors, particularly primary producers in obtaining credit facilities from the banks against the commodities stored by them. The functions of the Tamil Nadu Warehousing Corporation as laid down in the Warehousing Corporation Act, 1962 are to build godowns and warehouses at suitable places with prior approval of the State Government for storage and distribution of agricultural and notified commodities.

The authorised share capital of the corporation is Rs. 800/-lakhs. The paid up share capital of the corporation is Rs. 761/- lakhs out of which, the Central Warehousing Corporation has contributed Rs. 380.50 lakhs. In view of the good performance of the corporation during the year 1996-97, the gross income earned by the corporation during 1996-97 amounted to Rs. 839.66 lakhs as against the gross income of Rs. 771.94 lakhs during 1995-96. The profit of the year 1996-97 has also increased to Rs. 232.99 lakhs as against Rs. 204.27 lakhs in 1995-96. The net profit arrived at is Rs. 147.71 lakhs in 1996-97 as against Rs. 102.56 lakhs in 1995-96. For the year 1996-97 the Corporation declared a dividend of 3% on the paid up share capital which works out to Rs. 22.83 lakhs.

The storage space available in the warehouses of Tamil Nadu, various depositors utilize warehousing Corporation including Government agencies such as TNCSC, TNTBC, TNBSC Corporations, Fertilizer Manufacturing Companies, Cement Consuming Departments and other Private Depositors. The

Corporation has 246 owned godowns in 54 centres and 12 hired godowns in 10 centres. The detailed storage capacity and its utilization are furnished below.

As on 31.3.1998	MTs
Storage capacity (owned)	5,98,210
Storage capacity (Hired)	25,622
Total	6,23,832

Percentage of occupancy: 92%

During the year 1997 the occupancy status was 66%. Effective steps were taken to improve business yielded results and occupancy has risen to 92%. [12]

Procurement

To bridge the gap between the demand and supply of rice under PDS this Government makes local procurement of paddy especially in Cauvery Delta Areas, where production of paddy is abundant. The Government resorts to any one of the following methods after taking into consideration of various factors, such as area of cultivation, crop prospects, rainfall and productivity.

(i) Monopoly Procurement System: Only the Government Agency makes procurement and no private trader is allowed to procure paddy in the notified areas.

(ii) Parallel Procurement: Farmers have the option to sell their paddy either to the Government Agency or to the private traders at a price advantages to them.

(iii) Traders Levy System: Under this system, the traders who procure paddy or rice, could move the stock to the place of business only after tending the levy fixed by the Government from time to time.

The Government resort to anyone of the firsts two methods namely parallel monopoly since our past experience have proved that Traders Levy System has not given the desired results considering the time, energy and cost involved. During the last Kuruvai season 1.63 lakh M.Ts of paddy were procured under parallel procurement system.

Table 2.8

Procurement of Paddy in Tamil Nadu

(in Lakhs Tonnes)

Year	*Procurement of Paddy*	*Year*	*Procurement of Paddy*
1989	10.69	1994	6.38
1990	13.86	1995	3.39
1991	13.72	1996	2.45
1992	18.35	1997	16.48
1993	15.48	1998	11.86

Source: Government of Tamil Nadu, 1999.

About 10.84 lakh M.Ts of paddy have been procured under monopoly system, which was withdrawn by the Government with effect from 21.3.2000 in Cauveri delta. The system is being introduced in Cauvery Delta Areas, which comprises of 38 taluks in 8 districts out of 206 taluks in 29 districts. From 21.3.2000 onwards, parallel procurement system has been introduced in Cauvery Delta Areas because of the comfortable stock position of paddy/ rice and procurement under the system is about 5000 M.Ts per day. As on 15.4.2000, about 11.67 lakh M.Ts of paddy have been procured under current samba procurement operations.

With a view to encourage the farmers to sell paddy to the Government Agency and to secure good return to the farmers, an incentive by way of incidental charge ranging from Rs. 35/- to Rs. 50/- per quintals is being given to the farmers, over and above the minimum support price for paddy depending on the procurement system introduced during the last samba 99 season, the Government gave an incentive of Rs. 50/- per quintal, over and above the minimum support price fixed by the Government of India for paddy under monopoly procurement system and in last Kuruvai '99 season, an incidental charge as Rs. 35/- per quintal over and above minimum sport price was given under parallel procurement System.[13]

Even though the Government of India revised the issue price of rice allotted from the central pool, frequently, the state Government have been maintaining the issue price distributed through PDS to the level that existed in the year 1995. In fact, the Government has reduced the issue price of PDS rice from Rs. 3.75/- to 3.50/- per kg. with effect from 1.1.2000.

The table shows the Central Government issue prices and states government issue prices. The central government issue prices is Rs. 375/- per quintal but state government has shared equal amount of Rs. 700/- per quintal on issue prices of the commodity.

With the reintroduction of parallel procurement system in Cauvery Delta Areas, the number of Direct Purchase Centres that functional and the quantity of paddy procured in Kuruvai'97 season and number of Direct Purchase Centres that are functioning and quantity of paddy procured as on 31-3-98 during Samba'98 are as follows.

The procurement of paddy in various Districts and Taluks of Tamil Nadu, are: Thanjavur, Nagai, Thiruvarur,

Table 2.9

Comparison of Government of India Issue Price and State PDS Price

(price in Rs. per quintal)

Year	*Government of India price*	*State PDS price*
1983-84	215	235
1984-85	215	235
1985-86	244	250
1986-87	250	266
1987-88	250	279
1988-89	250	325
1989-90	350	370
1990-91	320	370
1991-92	350	458
1992-93	350	518
1993-94	475	648
1994-95	475	648
1995-96	375	648
1996-97	375	648
1997-98	375	700
1998-99	375	700

Source: Government of Tamil Nadu, 2000.

Cuddalore, Trichy, Pudukottai, Karur and Perambalur. Among eight Districts a higher procurement of paddy was handled only in Tanjavur District and Tiruvarur District of Tamil Nadu. Nearly 3,10,000 Million Tonnes in Tanjavur and 3,00,000 Million Tonnes of paddy procured from these districts.

To store the essential and other commodities, the TNCS corporation has created a storage capacity of 6,06,970 tonnes in 124 Taluks in 148 places. During 1997-98 the Government have issued orders for the constructions of 3 godowns in Kulithalai in Karur District, Sivagiri in Thirunelveli District and Pallipattu in Thiruvallur District at an estimated cost of Rs. 30 lakhs per godown. The corporation also hires godowns from Tamil Nadu Warehousing Corporation and others for its further requirements.

The Tamil Nadu Civil Supplies Corporation is having 23 Modern Rice Mills (MRM) at present. The paddy procured during kuruvai and samba season every year is hulled in the MRMs of the corporation. The total capacity is 1744 tonnes per day. The proposals for modernisation of Modern Rice Mills of Kallakrichi, Akkur, Thiruvarur and Chidambaram to increase the hulling capacity are under active consideration of the Government. The Tamil Nadu Civil Supplies Corporation has appointed 188 hulling agents and 148 custom-hulling agents. Their hulling capacity is 1.26 lakh tonnes per month.

Short weightment is the main problem among the major problems faced in Public Distribution System. In order to ensure correct weightment at the time of issue by the wholesaler (viz) new ones have replaced Tamil Nadu Civil Supplies Corporation to the retailers, the old 406 platform scales. The loss, on account of the implementation of the Government' policy on issue rice at less than economic cost through PDS and P.T.M.G.R. The Government of Tamil Nadu is regularly reimbursing nutritious Meal Programme to the corporation. The Government subsidy of Rs. 440 crores released in 1994-95 rose to Rs. 1000 crores in the year 1997-98. The subsidy is

Table 2.10

Procurement of Kuruvai and Samba in Tamil Nadu

		Kuruvai'97		Samba'98	
Sl. No.	Name of the District	No. of DPCs opened	Qty. of paddy procured MTs	No. of DPCs sanctioned	Qty of paddy procured as on 31-3-99. M.ts
1.	Thanjavur	195	2,28,541	287	3,06,934
2.	Nagai	94	1,37,529	177	1,96,773
3.	Thiruvarur	154	2,00,490	262	2,83,806
4.	Cuddalore	35	42,298	90	93,088
5.	Trichy	25	27,083	21	3,616
6.	Pudukottai	13	16,685	52	59,332
7.	Karur	—	—	7	1,460
8.	Perambalur	10	4,902	22	11,529
Total		526	6,57,528	918	9,56,538
Total Taluk Godown Purchase		—	47,239	—	36,644
D.P.C in other Districts		—	—	—	47,454
Grand Total		—	7,04,767	—	10,40,136

Source: Government of Tamil Nadu, 2000.

excepted to come down to Rs. 900 crores during current year owing to introduction of new PDS with new family cards.

During the year 1996-97 Bonus was sanctioned at 8.33% and ex-gratia of 10.67% to the C and D category employees working in TNCSC Limited. A sum of Rs. 825

as special Adhoc Bonus plus Rs. 1675/- Festival Advance was sanctioned to the B category employees of the corporation. The above amount was paid during the year 1997-98. The Government has already issued orders of the permanency of the load man who was working in the corporation for more than 10 years under certain norms. Civil Supplies Corporation is taking action to regularize their employees.

The vigilance cell of TNCSC had four teams functioning under the control of the vigilance officer. The vigilance teams make surprise inspection and on information about malpractice, acts on by inspecting filed points such as godowns, ration-shops, modern rice mills, DPCs, Railheads, Hulling centres etc., Disciplinary action, Recovery Proceedings are initiated against the earning staff and follow-up action is closely monitored by the vigilance cell.[14]

Distribution Performance

Scale of Supply

The objective of the Public Distribution System (PDS) is to make available certain essential commodities to the people of Tamil Nadu at easily accessible locations, at prices that are affordable and of a quality that is acceptable. At present, the Government is distributing rice; wheat, sugar, edible oils and kerosene under PDS through Fair Price Shop (FPS) located in each revenue village in the state.

The PDS in Tamil Nadu (Table. 2.11) cater to about 1.56 crores card holders through a massive network of Cooperative/TNCSC run FPS numbering 26515 both in rural and urban areas. A total quantity of rice distributed

Table 2.11

Present Scale of supply of Essential Commodities Public Distribution System in Tamil Nadu

Name of the commodity	*Scale of Supply*
Rice: Fine	Month subject to a minimum 12 kgs and
Common	Maximum of 20 kgs per month per card
Wheat	10 kgs per card in Chennai city and District Head quarters and other areas 5 kgs per card\per month
Sugar	500 gms per head per month maximum 2 kgs per card per month
Sooji	Maximum 2 kgs per card per month
Maida	Maximum 5 kgs per card per month
Palmolin Oil	1 litre per card
Kerosene	15 Litres for Municipalities 10 Litres for Township 5 Litres for Rural areas

Source: Policy Note on Food, Civil Supplies and Consumer Protection, Co-operation, Food and Consumer Protection Department Demand no: 34, Government of Tamil Nadu-1999.

during the last year has been 2208013 M.Ts. With an average monthly off-take of sugar/wheat and wheat products/kerosene/for the last year has been 26660 M.Ts/ 9226 M.Ts/3044 M.Ts/76421 KLs respectively.

Family Cards

With a view to ensuring availability of PDS commodities to all families throughout the state, the Government had implemented the computerized family card system on option basis, instead of categorizing families of Below Poverty Line (BPL) and Above Poverty

Line (APL). The new family card is designed in such a manner that the photo of the head of the family has been scanned and printed with the name of the family members, age and address and with shop details etc.

Number of family cards in circulation in the state prior to 1998 was 1.48 crores. New family cards have been issued from May 1998. As on 31.03.2000, over 1.56 crores family cards have been issued. A part of the increased number can be explained by the emergence of new households, however a part of it could be due to existence of bogus cards. It has been the endeavour of the Government to eliminate the bogus cards in the interest of providing adequate and effective service to the people through the PDS and to avoid leakages.

Each family card not only involves commitment on the part of the Government to supply the essential commodities to the cardholders but also a financial subsidy of about Rs. 2500 per card per annum. Therefore, the Government is very keen on identifying and eliminating bogus cards, while ensuring that the genuine households are not denied new cards. The Table 2.12 expressed the number of cards are circulated in Tamil Nadu. [15]

An option has been given to the cardholders to accept 3 kilos of sugar in lieu of rice and so far 11,17,709 sugar cards have been issued. Similarly another option has been given to the cardholders to accept 5 litres of kerosene in lieu of rice numbering 12,42,432 cards. 25796 kerosene cards have been issued to police personnel.

Fair Price Shop

Tamil Nadu is the only state where Fair Price Shops (FPS) are exclusively run either by the co-operatives or by

Table 2.12
Number of Cards in Tamil Nadu

Year	*No. of Cards (in Lakhs)*
1979-80	106.00
1980-81	108.98
1981-82	118.88
1982-83	119.10
1983-84	119.44
1984-85	119.60
1985-86	128.00
1986-87	NA
1987-88	120.00
1988-89	128.57
1989-90	126.71
1990-91	123.42
1991-92	123.42
1992-93	150.00
1993-94	150.00
1994-95	150.00
1995-96	150.00
1996-97	150.00
1997-98	150.00
1998-99	149.00
1999-2000	156.00

Source: Government of Tamil Nadu, 1999.

the TNCSC. The co-operatives through their network of co-operative wholesale stores; lead and link societies have been running 25,406 FPS. The TNCSC is running 1109 shops. The number of FPS has increased to 26,515 in 1999 from 23,125 FPS in 1996. The increase in the number of shops over the years is given below.

Table 2.13

Number of Ration Shops in Tamil Nadu

Year	*Urban*	*Rural*	*Total*	*TNCSC Shops*
1990-91	N.A	N.A	20,198	946
1991-92	N.A	N.A	20,907	946
1992-93	3547	17374	20,921	946
1993-94	4384	16528	20,912	946
1994-95	4384	16528	20,912	946
1995-96	5753	17206	22,959	946

Source: District Supplies Office, Dindigul 2000.

Out of these 26515 shops, 20626 shops are in rural areas and 5889 Shops in urban areas. The policy of the Government is to have at least one FPS in each revenue village. The District Collector have already been empowered to open FPS as per the guidelines prescribed. No cardholders should travel more than 2 kms and maximum number of cards attached to a shop should not exceed 800 in the case of urban areas and 500 in the case of rural areas. Retail outlets are opened by women Groups to distribute PDS commodities to the public, who need to walk beyond 2 kms to reach the allocated shops and the existing FPS has more number of family cards, there are also 36 Mobile shops in order to cater to the people in selective hill areas.

Storage Facility

In order to cater to the monthly requirements of the PDS of over 2 lakh tonnes of rice, 30,000 tonnes of wheat and 24000 tonnes of sugar, there exists a well built Godown network right from Taluk level. There are about 228 Godown totally, owned by Tamil Nadu Civil Supplies

Corporation Limited (141) Tamil Nadu Warehousing Corporation (54) Control Warehousing Corporation (20) and Food Corporation of India (13) with a total capacity of 23.24 lakh tonnes.

SUPPLY

The government is supplying the PDS commodities like, Rice, Sugar, Wheat Rava, Maida, Kerosene and Palmolin Oil etc.

Table 2.14

Supply of PDS Commodities in Tamil Nadu

(in Metric Tonne)

Commodity	*1993-94*	*1994-95*	*1995-96*
Rice	1102318	867582	1593083
Sugar	225558	195178	262899
Wheat	110964	63176	97979
Kerosene	496914	473333	657943
Palmolin oil	1346	6243	2679
Rava	N.A	N.A	16819
Maida	N.A	N.A	9275
Total	1936100	1605512	2640667

Source: Government of Tamil Nadu, 2000.

RICE

Rice is the staple food of the state and hence the Government attaches almost importance to ensure adequate stock of rice both at macro and micro levels, so that, the card holders do not suffer for want of rice in PDS outlets. The state requirements for PDS and other welfare measures are about 2.15 lakh tonnes per month. The monthly allocation of the Government of India was

1.09 lakh tonnes per month up to June 1999. Due to persistent efforts taken by the Hon'ble Chief Minister, it has been possible to obtain additional allocation of 50,000 metric tonnes quantity required for PDS/OAP/NMP i.e., 50,000 M.Ts is met by our own procurement through TNCSC Limited. [16]

Table 2.15

Rice-Off takes Under PDS in Tamil Nadu

(in lakh Tonnes)

Year	Rice	Year	Rice
1984	6.98	1992	14.70
1985	11.04	1993	14.30
1986	9.24	1994	12.80
1987	11.87	1995	13.72
1988	13.04	1996	24.13
1989	14.57	1997	22.20
1990	12.33	1998	21.48
1991	17.31	1999	22.08

Source: Policy Note on Food, Civil Supplies And Consumer Protection, Co-operation, Food and Consumer protection Department, Demand No: 34, 2000.

Now, the Government of India has doubled the monthly BPL quota and has allotted 91,580 M.Ts at 5.90 per kg. For the APL category the Government of India are issuing a quantity of 38, 440 metric tonnes per month at the rate of Rs. 11.80 per kg. In all, Tamil Nadu will receive a quantity of 1,30,020 M.Ts of rice under the above two categories from the Government of India. It is to be noted the central issue price will henceforth be based on the economic cost of the FCI, which is bound to fluctuate upward from time to time.

Because of the revised policy of the Government of India, the State Government will have an additional subsidy of about Rs. 300 crores per annum for rice distribution. Under earned by the stiff hike announced by the Government of India, the State Government have decided to continue to supply PDS rice at the existing rate of Rs. 3.50 per kg and a maximum of 20 kilos per card as before without passing on the burden to the consumer, so that the family cardholders particularly the poor and vulnerable sections are not but to any undue hardship. The Government Issue price is increased from Rs. 215 per quintal in 1983-84 to Rs. 375 in 1998-99. But state PDS price is increased from Rs. 235 to Rs. 700 during period from 1983-84 to 1998-99.

The gap between the issue price of rice in PDS and the cost of price of rice obtained from FCI and the loss incurred by the TNCSC in our local procurement area met by State Government by means of subsidy. For 2000-2001 a sum of Rs. 17000 crores has been provided for rice subsidy.

Table 2.16

Total subsidies released by Government of Tamil Nadu to T.N.C.S.C. Ltd. Towards loss incurred in Subsidies Distribution of Rice through PDS

Year	*Subsidies (Rs in crores)*	*Year*	*Subsidies (Rs in Crores)*
1984-85	63.90	1992-93	332.24
1985-86	79.00	1993-94	351.68
1986-87	65.00	1994-95	400.00
1987-88	117.61	1995-96	440.00
1989-90	184.53	1996-97	800.00
1990-91	208.79	1997-98	1000.00
1991-92	219.31	1998-99	1000.00

Sources: Government of Tamil Nadu, 1999..

The government wants to reduce food subsidy by increasing issue price and increasing the quantities under PDS. The quantity of cereals for the BPL families has been increased from 10 kgs to 20 kgs. This would have raised food subsidy by 100 crores. This may not materialise because with the increase in issue prices, the demand for PDS may get reduced and stocks with the government will more or less remain the same. The Table 3.16 shows the cost of Food increased from Rs 63.90 crores to Rs 1000 crores in the period from 1984-85 to 1998-99. The supply of PDS commodities increased from the year by year in Tamil Nadu.

WHEAT

Wheat is issued through the PDS at the rate of 10 kg per family card per month in Chennai City and Belt Areas and other District Headquarters and at 5 kg in the rest of the areas in the state. The entire requirements for PDS wheat are met from the central allocation. The Government of India is allotting 30,000 M. tonnes of wheat either under at APL or BPL allotment every month to the state at Rs. 705 per quintal at open market sales scheme rates with effect from 16.2.2000. Out of 30,000 M.Ts of wheat, 15000 M.Ts. was earmarked her distribution through PDS outlets and the remaining 15,000 M.Ts. to the Roller Flour Mills under custom Milling Scheme for extraction of wheat products viz. Rava and Maida for distribution under PDS. However, the Government of India has again revised the issue price of wheat to Rs. 9.00 per kg, which is the electronic cost of FCI. Accordingly the Tamil Nadu Government has revised the price of wheat and wheat products on 13-4-2000 as detailed in Table 2.17.

Under the revised guidelines issued by the Government of India on Targeted Public Distribution

Table 2.17

Price of Wheat and Wheat Products

Commodity	*Per kg* *Rs. P.*
Wheat	9.75
Rava	12.80
Maida	12.30

Source: Government of Tamil Nadu, 2000.

System with effect from 1.4.2000, no wheat is being allotted to the state at BPL rate. This Government has to obtain wheat from the Government of India only at APL rate (Economic costs). Since there is no appreciable difference in the price, the off-take in PDS is very low. Hence, the State Government has requested the Government of India to allot wheat to this state under BPL Rate. [17]

SUGAR

Sugar is issued under Public Distribution System at the rate of 500 grams per head subject to a maximum of 2 kg per Family Card per month. In view of the fact that option based Family Card System has been introduced, the cardholders, who have opted for sugar in lieu of rice will get 3 kg of sugar over and above their regular entitlement. Every year additional quantity of 1 kg of sugar is issued to all the cardholders during Deepavali Festival. As per the census 1991, the Population of Tamil Nadu was 5.57 crores and the number of households was 1.25 crores. On this basis, the Government of India has been allotting 23741 M.Ts. of levy sugar at the rate of 425 grams per head to this state.

For meeting the full requirements of sugar to all the cardholders including option based sugar cardholders, a minimum of 31,000 M.Ts of sugar per month is necessary. The average monthly off take of sugar is about 27,000 M.Ts. The Government of India have been requested by this Government to allot at least 27,000 M.Ts to meet the gap in between to demand and supply of sugar. Meanwhile, the TNCSC has purchased non levy sugar of about 6400 M.Ts from the Tamil Nadu Co-operative Sugar Federation/Tamil Nadu Sugar Corporation to meet the full requirements. The projected Population as on 1.3.99 for this state as estimated by the Government of India is 6.125 crores. The Government of India therefore increased the allotment to 26,033 M.Ts per month from 1.3.2000.

The Government of India also indicated that the income tax assessee and their family members would not be eligible for getting sugar under the PDS. The government already clarified that the existing system of distributing sugar under PDS would continue without excluding income tax assessee and their family members and that the option based sugar cardholders would continue to draw additional quantity of 3 kg sugar in the state. The retail price of the sugar issued through PDS has been revised as per the instructions of the Government of India from Rs. 12/- to Rs. 13/- per kg. with effect from 03-03-2000.

KEROSENE

The scale of supply of kerosene to the family card holders is given in Table 2.18.

The scale of supply of kerosene to the LPG cylinder holders has been restricted based on the instruction of the Government of India. In view of the fact that option based family card system has been introduced the card holders, who opted for kerosene will get 5 litres of kerosene over and above their regular entitlement. The number of card holders who opted for kerosene in lieu of rice is 12,47,432.

Table 2.18

Scale of Supply of Kerosene in Tamil Nadu

Places	*No. of LPG Connection*		
	Per cardholders Without LPG	*Single LPG*	*Double LPG*
Chennai City, District Head Quarters, Karaikudi, Husur, Kumbanakonam	10	3	
Other Municipalities	6	3	
Townships and Town Panchayats	5	3	
Rural Areas	3	3	
Nilgiris District Head Quarters	15	3	
Other Municipalities	15	3	
Townships and Town Panchayats	10	3	
Rural Areas	5	3	

Source: Government of Tamil Nadu, 2000.

Consequent on the increase in issue price of kerosene under PDS by the Government of India, retail-selling price has been fixed between Rs. 5.70 and Rs. 6.30 per litre depending upon the distance of the PDS outlets. Kerosene is also supplied through about 2924 handcart men, in the state. The requirements of kerosene including the option-based cards are 80539 KL per month. The Government of India is allotting 77108 KL of kerosene per month for distribution to family cardholders under PDS. There is a gap of about 3431-KL per month to meet 100% requirement under PDS. The Government of India have been moved to increase the allotment at least by 5% over and above the present allocation of 77108 KL per month with effect from 1.4.2000. The Government of India released an additional adhoc allotment of 400 KL during the month of September 1999 to this state and at the rate of 4000 KL per month from December 1999 to February 2000 for Elections and Cyclone in certain districts during the last monsoon.

Parallel Marketing System has been introduced in the state during November 1993. At present, 36 parallel marketers are in operation in the state with a network of 664 wholesalers and 8898 retailers as a consequence of which kerosene is now easily available in the open market. The scheme for establishment of kerosene Bunks like a control issuing bunk, ensuring accurate method of supply of kerosene to the cardholders on all working days, first ever in PDS is being implemented by this state. A kerosene bunk will serve about 8000 to 10000 family cards with in a radius of 2 kms, handling about 50 KL of kerosene for a month. A bunk will cost about Rs. 4.50 lakhs, out of which 50% is borne by the state Government as subsidy and the remaining would be met by the organizing institutions. [18] The progress of establishment in kerosene bunks is given in Table 2.19 below.

It has been proposed to establish 500 kerosene bunks throughout the state during the Ninth Five Year Plan period from 1997-2000. The Government propose to sanction a sum of Rs. 60.75 lakhs during 2000-2001.

PALMOLIN

Palmolin issued to all family cardholders at the rate of one litre per family card per month subject to availability. The Government of India has allotted palmolin to this state varying from 300 M.Ts to 500 M.Ts per month during the year 1999-2000 with effect from 27-7-1999. They reduced the central issue price of palmolin from Rs. 30, 000 to Rs. 20,000 per tonne in bulk. Based on the price revision made by the Government of India, the retail price for kerosene oil and Rs. 20/ per litre for pouched oil.

Table 2.19

Number of Kerosene Bunks in Tamil Nadu

		Number of kerosene bunk as on 31-3-2000						
Sl. No	*Particulars*	*Municipal Corporation*		*Municipalities*		*Town Panchayats*		*Total*
		Co-op	*TNCSC*	*Co-op*	*TNCSC*	*Co-op*	*TNCSC*	*Total*
1	**2**	**3**	**4**	**5**	**6**	**7**	**8**	**9**
1.	Total No. of Kerosene bunks functioning	54	20	87	4	36	—	201
2.	Ready for Inauguration	4	1	10	2	—	—	17
3.	Work in Progress	5	3	7	2	5	—	22
4.	Land acquired & work to be started	11	6	11	—	8	—	36
5.	Site identified but land to be acquired	3	4	12	—	—	—	24
6.	Site yet to be identified	62	—	—	—	—	—	62
	Total	139	34	127	8	54	—	362

Source: Government of Tamil Nadu. 2000.

The price of palmolin purchase in open market is around Rs. 24 to Rs. 25 per litre. The cost price of palmolin sold in the PDS is marginally high because of the issue price of the Government of India to reduce the central issue of palmolin further.[19]

Based on the analysis of performance of PDS in Tamil Nadu as discussed in the present chapter, a micro level analysis has been made in the study district-Dindigul District of Tamil Nadu and the results are interpreted in the forthcoming chapter.

REFERENCES

1. Government of India, Foodgrains (Future and Option Prohibition) order, dated 18 May 1942.
2. Government of India: Report of the Food grains Policy Committee, 1993. p. 4.
3. Government of India, "Report of the Committee on Control and Subsidies", Ministry of Finance, New Delhi, 1999.
4. Economic Survey, 1995-96.
5. Vyas, 1993.
6. Upadhyay, "Inflation, Food Security and Public Distribution System, "Social Action, Vol. 6. No. 3, July-September 1996.
7. Economic Survey, 1996-97.
8. Social Summit, Copenhasen. 1995.
9. R. Radhakrishnan, K. Subba Rao and et al. "*Indias Public Distribution System:* A National and International Perspectives", World Bank Discussion Paper. No. 380. World Bank, Washington. 1997.
10. Jos Mooij. E, "Public Distribution System as safety net: Who is saved?", Economic and Political Weekly, 1994.
11. Department of Food and Civil Supplies, Chennai. 2000.

12. State Trading Corporation. Chennai, 2000.

13. Policy Note on Food, Civil Supplies and Consumer Protection, Co-operation, Food and Consumer Protection Departments Demand No: 34, Government of Tamil Nadu 1999.

14. Office Records. Tamil Nadu Civil Supplies Corporation Limited, Chennai 2000.

15. Policy note on Food and Civil Supplies and Consumer Protection. Co-operation, Food and Civil Supplies Protection Department, Demand No: 34, Government of Tamil Nadu 2000.

16. Policy Note on Food, Civil Supplies and Consumer Protection, "Co-operation, Food and Consumer Protection Department", Demand No: 34, Government of Tamil Nadu, 1999.

17. Department of Food and Civil Supplies and Department of Consumer Protection, Chennai 2000.

18. Tamil Nadu Civil Supplies Corporation, Chennai. 2000.

19. Policy Note on Food, Civil Supplies and Consumer, Protection, Co-operation, Food and Consumer Protection, Government of Tamil Nadu, Demand No: 34, 2000.

3

Economic Reforms and Public Distribution System

The present chapter analyses the data (both secondary and primary) collected from the Dindigul district regarding organisation structure of PDS in Dindigul district, physical and financial performance of PDS before and after implementation of New Economic Policy and the impact of economic reforms on PDS etc. The secondary data regarding allotment, supply, prices, off-take, distribution of essential commodities through fair price shops and number of fair price shops, card holders etc., collected from District Supplies Office. Tamil Nadu Civil Supplies Corporation (TNCSC), Taluk Supply Office (TSO), Co-operative Office and District Collectorate are analysed in the first part of this chapter. Primary data regarding socio-economic status of beneficiaries and non-beneficiaries, details about awareness and use of PDS by the poor people and practical difficulties faced by the PDS beneficiaries are also analysed in detail in the second section of this chapter. A few hypotheses are also tested with suitable statistical analysis in this chapter.

Public Distribution System in Dindigul District

Organisational Structure

The cooperatives play a predominant role in the distribution of essential commodities to 4.43 lakh cardholders in Dindigul District. Essential commodities of mass consumption like rice, sugar, wheat, wheat products like rava and maida, edible oil and kerosene are distributed through five lead societies and 509 link societies by an extensive network of 613 FPS. The unique features of PDS in Tamil Nadu that no private traders are given license to run the FPS. At least one FPS is provided to each revenue village even the card strength is very low. The conveniences of the cardholders are given the highest priority. Even though every revenue village has FPS, there may be still certain areas, which are far away from the existing shop, and it may not be easily accessible to these villages. Because of the limited number of cards in remote areas there is necessary to open part time FPS. The District Collectors are empowered to permit the same after obtaining the concurrence of the Registrar of Cooperative Societies. There are 83 part time shops as on the date in the District.

The District Collector is coordinating the PDS activities at the district level by holding meeting with Civil Supplies Officials, Regional Managers of the Tamil Nadu Civil Supplies Corporation. Regional Joint Registrars, Deputy Registrar (PDS) and special officers of the lead societies, Secretary to Government also Commissioner of Civil Supplies, Chairman-cum-Managing Director of the Tamil Nadu Civil Supplies Corporation, Registrar of Cooperative Societies and the Inspector General of Police Civil Supplies. The organisational structure of PDS in Dindigul District is exhibited in Figure 3.1.

FIGURE 3.1

Channels of Distribution of Food Grains In Dindigul District

District Level Organisational Structure of the Public Distribution System

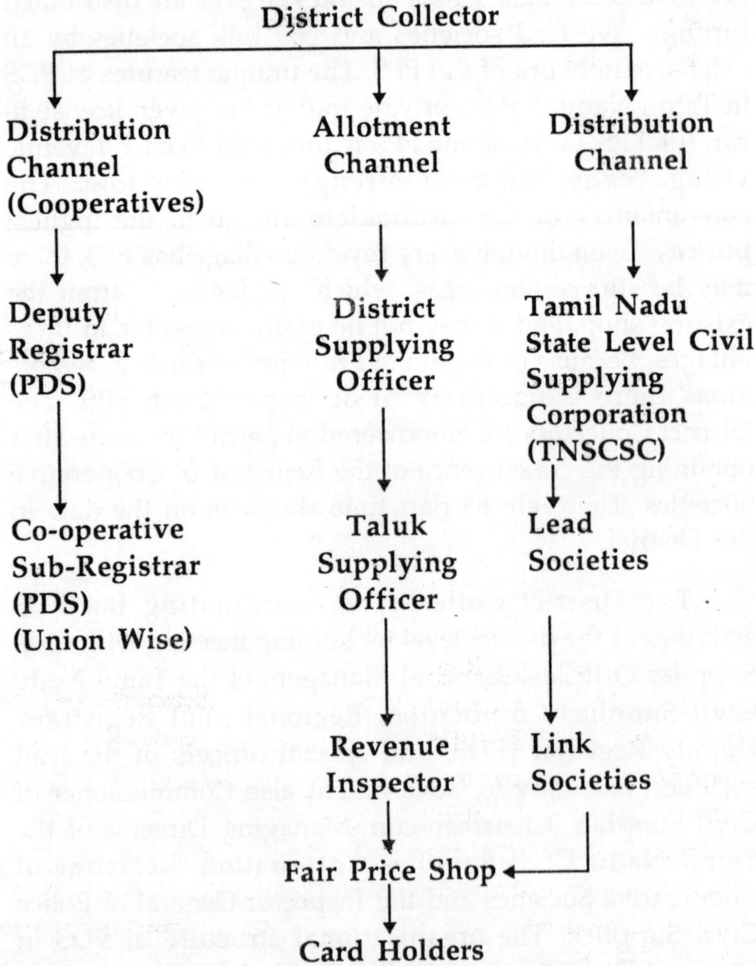

Source: Tamil Nadu Civil Supplies Corporation, Dindigul. 2000.

There are five lead societies in Dindigul district. They are:

1. Dindigul District Consumer Cooperative Whole Sale Society.
2. Palani Cooperative Marketing Society.
3. Kodaikanal Cooperative Stores,
4. Dindigul District Cooperative Marketing Society,
5. Southern Railway Employees Cooperative Stores

ALLOTMENT

The Commissioner of Civil Supplies allotted commodity based on standard allotment as per card. The present requirement of commodity is as per unit and per family card prevailing norms for the entire District and Taluk. Any family having card with three and more members will get 12 kg of rice. The State Government had ordered the supply of 20 kg rice even though the same would cost the Government an addition expenditure of Rs. 100 crores per annum. This scheme should be effectively implemented without any hesitation and hindrance. Giving free rice to the Old Age Pensioner (OAP), physically handicapped persons are some of the other activities of PDS System.

Table 3.1 reveals the limits of supply of PDS commodities to the cardholders in the year 1986-87 and 1995-96 in Dindigul District. In 1995-96 after implementation of New Economic Policy, rice was supplied at the rate of 12 kg per card. Sugar was supplied at 500 gms to 1 unit. 1000 gms to 2 units, 1500 gms to 3 units, and 2000 gms to 4 units. Wheat was supplied at 10 kg per card in District Head Quarters and 5 kg per card to areas other than District Head Quarters. Rava was supplied at 2 kg per card and maida at 2 kg per card.

Kerosene was supplied at 10 litres per card in Corporation area, 5 litres in Township, 3 litres in Village area and Palmolin oil was supplied at 1 litre per card. In 1986-87, (Before implementation of New Economic Policy) except wheat all the other was same. The kerosene limit was increased from 5 litre to and 10 litres in Corporation areas. In rural areas, the wheat supplies were same as in the Town areas of Dindigul District.

Table 3.1
Limits of Supply of PDS Commodities to the Card Holders

Sl. No.	*Commodity*	*Limits* 1995-96	1986-87
1.	Rice	12 kg per card	12 kg per card
2.	Sugar	1 unit 500 gms	1 unit 500 gms
3.	Wheat	10 kg in District Head Quatres	5 kg Per Card
		5 kg per card in others	2 kg per card
4.	Rava	2 kg per card	2 kg per card
5.	Maida	2 kg per card	2 kg per card
6.	Kerosene	10 litre per card in Corporation	5 litre per card in Corporation
		5 litre per card in Township or Town Panchayat	3 litre per card in Township or Town Panchayat
		3 litre per card in Rural areas	2 litre per card in Rural areas
7.	Palmolin Oil	1 litres per card	1 litre per card

Source: Tamil Nadu Civil Supplies Corporations—Dindigul Region 2000.

PRICES

The successive raising of the support prices even as production is increasing, with the government buying up all that is offered at the price prevents any decline in open market prices that would have occurred but for the government intervention. This keeps the open market prices higher than what they would have been in the absence of the open-ended support operations. This makes food dealer to the poor, especially the rural poor who are not purchase of foodgrains and daily wages in the urban informal sector. This is especially distributing since the poor-buy most of the grain from the open market.

The impact of larger increase in administered prices vis-a-vis market price has already available on the levels of retail prices of the variety of cereals supplied through the PDS in the different states. Since the PDS is by and large catering to the urban population only, although fair price shop outlet prevalent in rural centres in selected months of lean and peak seasons of rice in Tamil Nadu. The retail prices and the implicit price of rice in Tamil Nadu are much higher than the Fair Price Shops prices for even the super fine variety of the cereal. The price of PDS commodities at issue prices and open market prices during the period from 1986-87 to 1995-96 in Dindigul District are analysed in Table 3.2.

It is clear from the table 3.2 that the prices of all essential commodities had increased during the period from 1986-87 to 1995-96. After implementation of New Economic Policy, the price of wheat had increased from Rs. 2.60 in 1991-92 to Rs. 4.50 in 1996-97 and the price of sugar had also increased from Rs. 5.25 to Rs. 9.05 during the same period. Since 1993-94 the Government

Table 3.2

PDS Prices of Essential Commodities in Dindigul Distrct (1986-87 to 1995-96)

(in Rs./per kg)

Commodity	*1986-87* *Rs.*	*1987-88* *Rs.*	*1988-89* *Rs.*	*1989-90* *Rs.*	*1990-91* *Rs.*	*1991-92* *Rs.*	*1992-93* *Rs.*	*1993-94* *Rs.*	*1994-95* *Rs.*	*1995-96* *Rs.*
1. Rice										
(*a*) Fine	2.40	2.40	2.40	3.00	3.00	3.50	3.50	3.75	3.75	3.75
(*b*) Common	1.50	1.75	1.75	2.00	2.00	2.00	2.00	2.00	2.00	2.00
2. Wheat	2.15	2.20	2.20	2.20	2.60	2.60	3.35	4.50	4.50	4.50
3. Sugar	4.40	4.40	4.40	5.25	5.25	5.25	6.90	9.05	9.05	9.05
4. Rava	4.50	4.50	4.50	5.00	5.00	5.00	5.50	6.50	6.00	6.00
5. Maida	4.00	4.00	4.00	4.40	4.40	3.30	5.50	6.10	6.50	6.50
6. Kerosene (per litre)	2.25	2.50	2.45	2.45	2.60	2.95	2.95	2.95	2.95	2.95
7. Palmolin Oil (per litre)	12.75	13.50	16.75	17.50	17.50	20.30	25.15	26.50	27.10	29.00

Source: District Supplies Office, Dindigul Collectorate, Dindigul, 1999.

had been purchasing the rice at Rs. 9.80 per kilogram but supplying to the cardholder for Rs. 3.75 only. This implies that more than 6 Rupees per kilogram loss to the government. In the case of kerosene and rice, there were no price changes in the period following the introduction of the New Economic Policy i.e. from 1991-92 to 1995-96. The Table 3.3 explains the open market prices of PDS commodities in Dindigul District during the period from 1986-87 to 1995-96.

Table 3.3 reveals that during the 10 years period (1986-87 to 1995-96) the prices of Fine Rice had increased from Rs. 4.10 to Rs. 4.60. Common Rice price had increased from Rs. 3.50 to Rs. 9.10, wheat price had increased from 3.25 to Rs. 7.80, sugar price had increased from Rs. 6.05 to Rs. 13.75, Rava price had increased from Rs. 5.30 to Rs. 11.00, Maida price had increased from Rs. 5.20 to Rs. 11.00, Kerosene price had increased from Rs. 5.50 to Rs. 9.60, and Palmolin oil price had also increased from Rs. 21.35 to Rs. 37.00 during the period from 1986-87 to 1995-96.

During the study period, while comparing the PDS prices of essential commodities of rice, sugar and kerosene and open market prices of Rice, sugar and kerosene, we could seen that there is great difference. In 986-87, PDS price of Rice was Rs. 2.40 and open market price of Rice was Rs. 4.10, that of sugar was Rs. 4.40 and Rs. 6.05 and of kerosene was Rs. 2.25 and open market prices was Rs. 5.50. In 1995-96 the PDS price of Rice was Rs. 3.75 and in open market price of rice was Rs. 9.60 that of sugar was Rs. 4.50 and Rs. 13.75 and kerosene was Rs. 2.95 and Rs. 9.60. The essential commodities of Rice, Sugar and Kerosene at PDS price level were lower than the open market prices.

Table 3.3

Open Market prices of (PDS) Commodities in Dindigul District 1986-87 to 1995-96

(in Rs./per kg)

Commodity	*1986-87* *Rs.*	*1987-88* *Rs.*	*1988-89* *Rs.*	*1989-90* *Rs.*	*1990-91* *Rs.*	*1991-92* *Rs.*	*1992-93* *Rs.*	*1993-94* *Rs.*	*1994-95* *Rs.*	*1995-96* *Rs.*
1. Rice										
(*a*) Fine	4.10	4.40	5.00	5.25	5.50	6.40	6.40	6.60	8.40	9.60
(*b*) Common	3.50	3.60	3.80	4.00	4.80	5.10	5.80	5.40	8.25	9.10
2. Wheat	3.25	3.40	4.05	4.75	4.90	6.80	6.70	7.80	6.50	7.80
3. Sugar	6.05	6.25	7.00	7.75	8.40	8.70	10.40	13.80	11.40	13.75
4. Rava	5.30	5.60	4.90	5.50	5.50	6.00	6.60	7.30	7.35	11.00
5. Maida	5.20	5.40	4.90	5.00	5.60	6.00	6.40	7.10	7.75	11.00
6. Kerosene (per litre)	5.50	5.75	5.80	6.00	6.10	6.20	6.00	6.00	6.40	9.60
7. Palmolin Oil (per litre)	21.35	22.00	22.60	23.10	27.00	29.50	31.00	32.50	35.00	37.00

Source: Assistant Directorate of Statistics Office, Dindigul Collectorate, Dindigul, 1999.

An analysis has been made to correlate the increase in price of PDS commodities and the changes in prices in open market. The hypothesis that there is positive relation between the increase of PDS prices and the prices of the commodities in open market. The prices of seven major commodities namely Rice Fine, Rice Common, Wheat, Sugar, Rava, Maida, Kerosene, Palmolin oil are analysed in this section. PDS prices and open market prices of the seven commodities have estimated for the period from 1986-87 to 1995-96 by using secondary data available in the Assistant Directorate of Statistics, Dindigul.

In order to find out the relationship between these two factors, coefficient of correlation is used. The coefficient of correlation is denoted by the symbol 'r' given by formula

R=XY

The correlation given in the equation has been used to find out the PDS and open market prices of seven commodities.

R = Coefficient of Correlation

X = dependent variable (PDS Price of fine rice, common rice, wheat, sugar, rava, maida, kerosene palmolin oil).

Y = independent variable (Open market price of fine rice, common rice, wheat, sugar, rava, maida, kerosene, palmolin oil). Given a random sample from a PDS and open market, we are to test the hypothesis that the correlation coefficient of the price is zero. i.e. the variables in prices are correlated; we have to apply the following.

t = r

t = test of significance

r = Correlation

't' test is used to find out the level of significance. The result is depicted in table 3.4.

Table 3.4

Correlation Between PDS and Open Market Prices of Seven Commodities

Sl. No.	*Commodity*	*'r'*	*Calculated 't' value*
1.	Fine rice	0.857	4.73**
	Common rice	0.695	2.72
2.	Wheat	0.852	4.57**
3.	Sugar	0.967	10.73**
4.	Rava	0.732	3.03
5.	Maida	0.790	3.63
6.	Kerosene	0.599	2.22*
7.	Palmolin Oil	0.966	10.55**

Source: Computed from the secondary data collected at Dindigul District Collectorate, 1999.

* Significant at 5 per cent level 't' 2.228

**Significant at 1 per cent level 't' 3.169.

From the table, it is observed that there is highly positive correlation between PDS and open market prices of fine rice, wheat, sugar, palmolin oil, viz., (0.857, 0.852, 0.967, 0.966). Since it is significant at 1 per cent and 5 per cent level, the calculated value of 't' is greater than the table value ('t' value viz., 4.73, 4.57, 10.73, 10.55) and hence the result of the experiences does not support the hypothesis that the variable in the price are highly correlated.

And the prices of common rice, rava, maida, kerosene are having low positive correlation between PDS and open market prices (correlation value viz., 0.695, 0.732, 0.790,

0.599). For the calculated value of 't' is greater than table value ('t' value viz., 2.72, 3.03, 3.63 and 2.22) and hence the result of the experiments does not support the hypothesis that the variables in the price are correlated.

STOCK OF FOODGRAINS

The recommended stock of foodgrains on 1st July of every year is 22.3 million tonnes. The Food Corporation of India had a foodgrain stock of 35.6 million tonnes in July 1995. FCI had on excess holding of about 7.72 million tonnes in 1994 and 13.4 million tonnes in 1995 which means that the carrying cost of buffer stocks would have increased by 45 per cent in 1994 and 78 per cent in 1995. Since the carrying cost of one tonne of foodgrains in 1994-95 was Rs. 1447, the extra stock would involve an additional Central Government expenditure of about Rs. 9689 million in 1994-95. Recently, the Central Government has permitted the FCI to off-load the foodgrain stocks of the prices fixed by it. The Table 3.5 explains the stock of foodgrains in Dindigul District during the period from 1986-87 to 1995-96.

Table 3.5 reveals that the Rice stock had increased from 10110.118 Tonne kilograms in 1986-87 to 13782.951 Tonne kilograms in 1995-96. The wheat stock increased from 38.125 Tonne kilograms to 399.589 Tonne kilograms during the same period. Similarly the stock of rava, kerosene and palmolin oil had also increased during the same period. But we see that sugar stock had decreased from 768.110 Tonne kilogram in 1986-87 to 226.747 Tonne kilo in 1995-96 and maida stock had also decreased from 5.884 tonne kg to 4.395 tone kg during the same period. It is inferred that due to price revision and some other

Table 3.5

Stock of Foodgrains of PDS in Dindigul District

(in Tonne Kilograms)

Commodity	1986-87	1987-88	1988-89	1989-90	1990-91	1991-92	1992-93	1993-94	1994-95	1995-96
1. Rice	10110.118	12567.414	4387.440	114.450	12928.436	9583.413	10130.524	16659.274	15730.739	13782.951
2. Wheat	38.125	42.506	126.900	908.933	955.686	1002.110	1223.698	410.869	465.106	399.589
3. Sugar	768.110	691.715	497.134	276.660	511.342	626.373	1060.376	277.675	275.976	226.747
4. Rava	2.418	3.543	1.644	2.167	0.661	0.660	0.660	0.773	6.537	4.395
5. Maida	5.884	7.783	4.440	14.719	2.815	2.800	2.800	2.801	5.539	4.395
6. Kerosene (in Tonne kilo litre)	1,176	5,842	2,290	21.525	9.401	10,112	24.183	15,614	6,196	14,865
7. Palmolin Oil (in Tk 1)	18,410	21,553	139,746	7,821	21,844	15,116	12,201	4,800	9,035	19,806

Source: Tamil Nadu Civil Supplies Corporation, Dindigul Region, Dindigul, 1999.

reason, the stock of essential commodities had increased after implementation of New Economic Policy.

SUPPLY OF FOODGRAINS

The Table 3.6 explains the supply of foodgrains in Dindigul District from 1986-87 to 1995-96. The data were collected from the office of Tamil Nadu Civil Supplies Corporation in Dindigul Region.

From Table 3.6 we infer that the Rice supplies increased from 34311.102 Tonne kilograms to 51226.986 tonne kilograms, sugar from 5958.167 tonne kilograms to 8168.474 tonne kilograms, Rava supplies increased from 80.163 tonne kilograms to 4053.208 tonne kilograms, kerosene supplies increased from 411.110 tonne kilo litre to 1851.258 tonne kilo litre but the supply of palmolin oil decreased from 110.720 tonne kilo litre to 72.776 tonne kilo litre and wheat decreased from 4799.621 tonne kgs to 2180.478 tonne kgs. Except wheat and palmolin supplies, all the remaining essntial commodities increased during the period.

FAIR PRICE SHOPS

The Government runs public distribution system through network of fair price shops, located in urban and rural all-over the country with the objective of making available foodgrains to the public at reasonable prices. The fair price shops are distributing the essential commodities to meet the day to day needs of the public. Table 3.7 shows the number of ration shop-taluk wise in Dindigul District.

It is seen that the large number of ration shops had increased from 440 in 1986-87 to 558 in 1995-96 in Dindigul District. After implementation of New Economic Policy, it had risen from 492 in 1991-92 558 ration shops in 1995-96. Large number of ration shops are functioning in Dindigul Taluk (180), Palani (87), Vedasandur (82),

Table 3.6

Supply of PDS Commodities in Dindigul District

(in Tonne Kilograms/Kilo litre)

Commodity	*1986-87*	*1987-88*	*1988-89*	*1989-90*	*1990-91*	*1991-92*	*1992-93*	*1993-94*	*1994-95*	*1995-96*
1. Rice	34311.102	3655.600	37512.301	38968.805	42119.607	615.813	54447.422	24684.380	40830.894	51226.986
2. Wheat	4799.621	4864.257	5012.607	4988.550	5508.819	6130.320	6920.080	1392.208	2732.395	2180.478
3. Sugar	5958.167	6115.413	6528.101	8437.279	8073.986	8180.135	8283.342	8437.656	8212.474	8168.474
4. Rava	1.00	1.011	1.300	1.581	1.551	25.880	212.130	567.626	479.036	725.780
5. Maida	80.163	110.624	112.453	46.276	11.809	397.643	1124.281	2442.800	2772.320	4053.208
6. Kerosene (Tonne kilo litre)	411.110	432.415	518.603	524.711	1488.891	1488.930	1488.945	1768.844	1822.238	1851.258
7. Palmolin oil	110.720	206.178	306.456	181.890	1054.306	900.600	180.882	201.675	247.290	72.776

Source: Tamil Nadu Civil Supplies Corporation Dindigul Region, Dindigul, 1999.

Table 3.7

Number of Ration Shops in Dindigul District

Sl. No.	Taluk	1986-87	1987-88	1988-89	1989-90	1990-91	1991-92	1992-93	1993-94	1994-95	1995-96
1.	Dindigul	138	138	150	152	154	154	155	169	172	180
2.	Nilakottai	54	54	55	57	59	60	60	62	62	63
3.	Natham	25	25	28	28	30	30	30	34	34	34
4.	Palani	75	75	78	78	79	79	80	85	86	87
5.	Ottanchatram	58	58	63	63	64	65	65	68	70	70
6.	Vedasenthur	60	60	65	16	70	70	72	75	78	82
7.	Kodaikkanal	17	17	18	18	18	20	23	25	26	26
8.	TNCSC*										
	Dindigul	8	8	8	8	8	8	9	9	9	9
	Kodaikanal	5	6	6	6	6	6	7	7	7	7
	Total	440	441	471	476	488	492	501	534	544	558

Source: District Supplies Office, Dindigul 2000

Note: *TNCSC 14 to 16 Shops and Maintained by Tamil Nadu Civil Supplies Corporation Limited Dindigul Region, Dindigul, 1999.

Table 3.8
Number of Ration Cards in Dindigul District

(in Number)

Sl. No.	Taluk	1986-87	1987-88	1988-89	1989-90	1990-91	1991-92	1992-93	1993-94	1994-95	1995-96
1.	Dindigul	116410	116970	115821	124015	125450	125560	126800	126000	127810	130500
2.	Nilakottai	43206	43105	42890	45726	47080	47460	47510	45866	47060	47250
3.	Natham	23980	24000	24167	24913	25698	25948	27850	26935	27080	27200
4.	Palani	44130	47880	48000	48517	49010	50186	50410	48180	49005	49506
5.	Ottanchatram	39885	40000	39810	39996	40726	40987	42837	42000	43400	43510
6.	Vedassandur	56672	56010	55600	55870	54300	55010	55080	54807	56614	58090
7.	Kodaikana	118217	18903	18476	18873	19150	20125	20550	20060	21325	21743
8.	TNCSC*										
	Dindigul	4795	4814	4927	4992	5010	5270	5210	5605	5800	5965
	Kodaikanal	3516	3652	3680	3741	3900	3998	4125	4310	4410	4510
	Total	3,50,811	3,55,334	3,53,374	3,66,642	3,70,324	3,74,444	3,80,372	3,73,763	3,82,114	3,88,274

Note: TNCSC* (Tamil Nadu Civil Supplies Corporation), Individually maintained from some shops in Dindigul Town and Kodaikanal.

Source: Dindigul Supplies Office, Collectorate, Dindigul, 1999.

Oddanchatram (70) and Nilakkottai (63). But the functioning of FPS in Natham and Kodaikkanal taluks is meagre in number.

Ration Cards

The Government of Tamil Nadu is trying to computerise the PDS system so as to weed out the bogus cards. Accordingly with the assistance from ELCOT and according to official estimates, out of the total 1.50 crore cards, 20 lakhs cards were bogus and people would cause a great loss to the government ex-chequer. The new ration cards would be distributed to the public in three phases. In the first phases, the new cards would be distributed in Chennai and the other Corporation areas, while Municipalities and the district headquarters would be taken up in the second phase, all the remaining areas-town and village panchayats would be covered in the third phase.

In Dindigul district, the number of ration cards was 3,50,811 in 1986-87 and it was increased to 3,88,274 cards in 1995-96. Of the total ration cards, the Dindigul taluk is having 1,30,500 cards (33.61 per cent). Similarly, Palani (49,506 cards), Vedasandur (58,090 cards), Nilakkottai (47,250 cards) taluks are dominating in the cards distribution in Dindigul District. Regarding the year wise growth performance of ration cards in Dindigul District, a slow growth in the total number of cards, after implementation of New Economic Policy, i.e., 3,80,372 cards in 1991-92 and 3,88,274 in 1995-96. Nearly 40,000 new cards were supplied to the Public within 10 Years in Dindigul District.

The state had 23,125 fair price shops of which 18,242 were in the rural areas and 4,883 shops were in the urban areas. Efforts were being made to have at least one PDS shop in every revenue village. In rural areas, the number of cards to be attached to each shop would range between

Table 3.9
Number of Ration Shops in Dindigul Taluk

Sl. No.	*Frika*	*1986-87*	*1990-91*	*1995-96*
1.	Dindigul Town	36	38	43
2.	Dindigul South	9	10	10
3.	Dindigul North	14	16	18
4.	Reddiyar Chathiram	6	8	10
5.	Palakkanoothu	10	11	14
6.	Dharmathupatti	5	6	9
7.	Athoor	14	17	19
8.	Chinnalapatti	18	19	21
9.	Sempatty	13	14	16
10.	Siluvathoor	5	6	8
11.	Kampliputhur	8	9	12
	Total	138	154	180

Source: Taluk Supplies Office, Dindigul, 1999.

500 and 800 and no consumer would be required to walk more than 2 kilometres to reach a shop. The number of ration shop function at Dindigul Taluk is exhibited in Table 3.9.

Table 3.9 explains the number of ration shops in Dindigul Taluk of Dindigul District. The number of ration shops in Dindigul Taluk are classified into 11 Frika, namely, 1. Dindigul Town, 2. Dindigul South, 3. Dindigul North, 4. Reddiyarchatram, 5. Palakkanoothu, 6. Dharmathupatti, 7. Athoor, 8. Chinnalapatti, 9. Sempatty, 10. Siluvathur, and 11. Kampliputhur. The total number of ration shops increased from 138 in 1986-87 to 180 in 1995-96 in the study period in Dindigul Taluk. A large number of ration shops is located in Dindigul Town Frika (urban) and Chinnalapatti Frika (Rural). The ration shops in Dindigul Town Frika increased from 36 to 43, and Chinnalapatti Frika ration shop increased from 18 to

Table 3.10
Number of Ration Cards in Dindigul Taluk

(in Number)

Sl. No.	Frika	1986-87	1987-88	1988-89	1989-90	1990-91	1991-92	1992-93	1993-94	1994-95	1995-96
1.	Dindigul Town	36380	36715	36423	37940	38068	39079	38563	38465	38958	39500
2.	Dindigul South	5885	5950	5815	6736	6892	6894	6915	6872	6880	7350
3.	Dindigul North	11793	11860	11865	11987	12524	12536	12580	12540	12685	12850
4.	Reddiyarchatram	5818	5998	5980	6100	67149	6110	6127	6127	6180	6460
5.	Palakhanoothu	7940	7950	7960	8413	8735	8740	8965	8882	8997	9680
6.	Dharmathupatty	5706	5740	5710	5878	5760	5795	5816	5748	5890	6000
7.	Athoor	7005	7196	7043	8680	8676	8693	8799	8797	8845	9000
8.	Chinnalapatty	13435	13985	13860	14915	15100	15108	15210	14798	15360	15400
9.	Sempatty	10810	11058	10080	11550	11012	11045	11250	11196	11225	11350
10.	Siluvathoor	4114	4100	4216	4738	4790	4797	4800	4800	4910	4960
11.	Kampliputhur	6456	6418	6965	7716	7744	7763	7775	7775	7680	7950
	Total	115342	116970	115824	124103	125450	125560	126800	126000	127810	130500

Source: Taluk Supplies Office, Dindigul, 2000.

21 during the same period in Dindigul Taluk of Dindigul District. The Frika wise distribution of Ration cards in Dindigul Taluk is given in Table 3.10.

Table 3.10 explains that the number of ration cards in Dindigul Taluk during the study period from 1986-87 to 1995-96 in Dindigul District. Dindigul Taluk classified into eleven (11) Frika. In Dindigul Taluk, ration cards were increased from 115342 in 1986-87 to 130500 in 1995-96. Nearly 16,000 new cards are distributed to the public during the same period of 10 years. A large number of Ration Cards were circulated in Dindigul Town Frika (urban) (39500 cards) and Chinnalapatty Frika (Rural) (15400 cards) in the year 1995-96 in Dindigul Taluk. The large number ration cards users are living in Dindigul Town Frika (Urban) and Chinnalapatti Frika (Rural) in Dindigul Taluk of Dindigul District. Primary data were also collected from the same Dindigul Taluk of Dindigul district.

Public Distribution System During Economic Reforms Period

The present section has been categorised into three parts. The first part explains the socio-economic conditions of respondents PDS beneficiaries and Non-PDS beneficiaries. The changes in income, expenditure and debt position of the respondents after implementation of NEP are analysed with the suitable statistical tools in the second part. The last part of this section discusses the opinion and awareness about PDS of the respondents. In order to analyse the real impact of PDS on poor in Dindigul district, a sample of 150 PDS beneficiaries and 150 non-PDS beneficiaries were interviewed. The result of the survey is analysed in this section.

Socio-Economic Conditions of Respondents

The socio-economic conditions are the deciding factors and they have a direct bearing on the ration cardholder and non-ration cardholders. Socio-economic conditions of the respondents are related to various factors like age, sex, community, religion, occupation, education, employment, assets and family size, etc. The respondents are classified into rural and urban households and the PDS beneficiaries with the non-PDS beneficiaries.

Table 3.11

Area-wise classification of the sample respondent

Sl. No.	*Area*	*PDS beneficiaries*		*Non-PDS beneficiaries*		*Total*
		Card holder	*Non-card holder*	*Card holder*	*Non-card holder*	
I.	Rural					
(i)	Perumalkovilpatti	15	10	25	—	50
(ii)	Chinnalapatti	25	—	—	25	50
(iii)	Chettiyapatti	25	—	6	19	50
II.	Urban					
(i)	Y.M.R. Patti	20	5	25	—	50
(ii)	Balakrishnapuram	25	—	45	21	50
(iii)	Trichi Road	20	5	—	25	50
	Total	130 (43.4)	20 (6.6)	60 (20.0%)	90 (30.0)	300 (100)

Source: Computed from the primary data.

Note: Figures within parenthesis denotes percentages.

Table 3.11 explains the area wise classification of the sample respondent. Of the 300 sample respondents, in the rural area, 75 respondents are beneficiaries and 75 respondents are non-beneficiaries. On the other hand in urban area, 75 respondents are beneficiaries and 75 are non-beneficiaries. The sample villages are Perumal Koilpatti, Chinnalapatti and Chettiyapatti. The sample urban area are Y.M.R. Patti, Balakrishnapuram and Trichy road in Dindigul town. Of the PDS Beneficiaries, 130 respondents are cardholders and 20 respondents are non-cardholders. Of the non-PDS Beneficiaries, 90 respondents are non-cardholders and 60 respondents are cardholders. It is inferred that 43.4 per cent of PDS beneficiaries are cardholders and 30.0 per cent of Non-PDS beneficiaries are non-card holders.

Age is an achieved characteristic in the life cycle of human being. Age plays a key role in determining the needs of the individuals. Needs identification, needs fulfilment and the process of need fulfilment are to a greater extent related to the age of the person concerned. Hence knowledge about age is essential to arrive at meaningful conclusion in these type of studies. An attempt is made to classify beneficiary and non-beneficiary sample respondents on the basis of age group and the same is summarised in Table 3.12.

In the rural area, the majority of the PDS Beneficiary households belongs to the age group between 41-50 years (28 respondents) followed by 31-40 years (20 respondents) The majority of the non-PDS beneficiary households belong to the age group between 31-40 years (25 respondents) followed 41-50 years (10 respondents). In urban area, the majority of the PDS respondents household belongs to the age group between 31-40 years (42 respondents), followed by 41-50 years (21 respondents). The majority of the non-PDS respondents belong to the age group between 31-40 years (36 respondents) followed by 41-50 years (24 respondents). From the table we conclude that 41.0 per cent of sample respondents (123 respondents) belongs to the age group between 31-40 years).

Table 3.12
Age-wise Classification of the Sample Respondent

Sl. No. No.	Age (Range)	Rural		Urban		Total	Percentage
		PDS Beneficiaries	Non-PDS Beneficiaries	PDS Beneficiaries	Non-PDS Beneficiaries		
1.	20-30	11	10	9	7	37	12.38
2.	31-40	20	25	42	36	123	41.0
3.	41-50	28	21	21	24	94	31.3
4.	51-60	16	14	2	8	40	13.4
5.	61 above	—	5	1	—	6	2.0
	Total	75	75	75	75	300	100.00

Source: Computed from the primary data.

Sex, the ascribed of human beings plays a dominant role in the life of the human beings. Especially in determining the status and performing certain roles and for even achieving certain positions because the various other factors such as values, traditions and cultures plays an integral role with this characteristic in deciding the features. Here in this study, the sex related with head of the household is analysed and the outcome is given Table 3.13.

Table 3.13 reveals that in rural area, 66 PDS beneficiary respondent are male and 9 are female and 65 non-PDS beneficiary respondent are male and 10 are female. In urban area, 67 PDS beneficiary respondent are male and 8 are female and 69 non PDS beneficiary respondent are male and 6 are female in the study district. Of the 300 respondents, 133 respondents (44.3 per cent) are male and 17 respondents (5.7 per cent) are female. In non-PDS beneficiaries, 134 respondents (44.7 per cent) are male and 16 respondents (5.3 per cent) are female. Thus, 92.3 per cent of respondents are male and 7.7 per cent of respondents are female in Dindigul District.

No man on this death will be without of any religion because it is assigned to him by his birth. It is of changing nature, also it is possible in a polycultural set up, whereas in a rural set up it possible so. Once a man is born in a religion means it is not so easy to move out of it. Again in a particular locality we are able to see the dominance of one single religion alone. Here the attempt is made to find out the religion of the study area and the derivation is given in Table 3.14.

Table 3.14 shows the religion wise classification of the sample respondents in Dindigul district. In Rural area, 64 PDS Beneficiaries and 72 non-PDS beneficiaries were Hindus. 11 PDS Beneficiaries and 2 Non-PDS Beneficiaries

Table 3.13

Sex-wise Classification of the Sample Respondent

Sl. No.	Area	PDS Beneficiaries			Non-PDS Beneficiaries			Total		
		Male	Female	Total	Male	Female	Total	Male	Female	Total
1.	Rural	66	9	75	65	10	75	131	19	150
2.	Urban	67	8	75	69	6	75	136	14	150
	Total	133 (44.3)	17 (5.7)	150 (50.0)	134 (44.7)	16 (5.3)	150 (50.0)	277 (92.3)	33 (7.7)	300 (100)

Source: Computed from the primary data.

Note: Figures parenthesis denotes the percentage.

Table 3.14

Religion—wise Classification of the Sample Respondent

Sl. No.	*Religion*	*Rural*		*Urban*		*Total*	*Percentage*
		PDS Beneficiaries	*Non-PDS beneficiaries*	*PDS beneficiaries*	*Non-PDS beneficiaries*		
1.	Hindu	64	72	50	61	247	82.3
2.	Christian	11	2	16	10	39	13.0
3.	Muslim	—	1	9	4	14	4.7
	Total	75	75	75	75	300	100.0

Source: Computed from the primary data.

were Christians and only 1 non-PDS Beneficiary was Muslim. In urban area, 50 PDS beneficiaries and 61 non-PDS beneficiaries were Hindus. 16 PDS beneficiaries and 10 Non-PDS beneficiaries were Christians and 9 PDS Beneficiaries and 4 non-PDS Beneficiaries were Muslims. It is clear that 82.3 percent of respondents (247) are belonging to Hindu religion, 13.0 per cent of respondents (39) are belonging to Christian religion and 4.7 per cent respondents (14) are belonging to Muslim religion.

In the social hierarchy the community to which a person plays a major role. The community is deciding factor for one's occupation, marriage and various other aspects in the life of an individual especially social mobility and social transformation.

Table 3.15 shows that in the rural area, 39 PDS beneficiary respondents and 24 non-PDS beneficiary respondents belong to SC/ST Community, 6 PDS respondents and 20 non-PDS respondents belong to MBC Community, 30 PDS respondents and 30 non-PDS respondents belong to BC community and only 1 respondent belongs to FC Community. In urban, 34 PDS respondents, and 15 non-PDS respondents belongs to SC/ST community, 13 PDS respondents and 17 PDS respondents belong to MBC community, 22 PDS respondents and 39 non-PDS respondents are belong to BC community and 6 PDS respondents 4 non-PDS respondents belongs to the FC community. It is inferred that of the 300 respondents, the 121 respondents (40.3 per cent) belongs to BC Community, 112 respondents (37.3 per cent) belongs to SC/ST community 56 respondents (18.7 per cent) belongs to MBC community and 11 respondents (5.7 per cent) belong to the FC community. Thus, majority of the sample respondents belongs to BC community (40.3 per cent) in study district.

Table 3.15

Community-wise classification of the sample respondent

Sl. No.	*Comm*	*Rural*		*Urban*		*Total*	*Percentage*
		PDS Beneficiaries	*Non PDS Beneficiaries*	*PDS beneficiaries*	*Non PDS Beneficiaries*		
1.	SC/ST	39	24	34	15	112	37.3
2.	MBC	6	20	13	17	56	18.7
3.	BC	30	30	22	39	121	40.3
4.	FC	—	1	6	4	11	3.7
	Total	75	75	75	75	300	100.00

Source: Computed from the primary data.

Education is an important factor, which decides the standard of living, level of participation in various activities and one's access to various aspects. Table 3.16 reveals the educational status of the sample respondents in Dindigul District. In the rural area, 14 PDS respondents and 17 non PDS respondents were illiterates. 44 PDS respondents and 40 non-PDS respondent had completed their primary education 17 PDS respondents and 18 non-PDS respondents had completed their secondary school education and non a single respondent had completed above school level. In the urban area, 8 PDS respondents and 1 non-PDS respondent were illiterates, 31 PDS respondent and 40 non-PDS respondents had completed their primary education, 28 PDS respondents and 18 non-PDS respondents were completed their secondary school education and only 8 PDS respondents had completed above school level.

Of the 300 sample respondents, 155 respondents (51.7 per cent) had completed primary education, 81 respondents (27.0 per cent) had completed secondary school level, 8 respondents (2.6 per cent) had completed above school level and 56 respondents (18.7 per cent) were illiterate in study district. Thus, 51.7 per cent of respondents constituted those who had completed primary education in Dindigul District and they formed the major share of the total respondents.

Each and every man on earth has to do some duty, for that he may be rewarded in terms of monetary benefits and kind. The occupational status is determined by ones educational and religious status because if one is having a higher status in education it means that the occupational status will be high. Here we are going to see two categories of occupation, namely blue and white colour. The occupational status of the respondents in the rural and urban areas is stated in Table 3.17.

Table 3.16

Educational Status of the Sample Respondents

Sl. No.	Level	Rural		Urban		Total	Percentage
		PDS Beneficiaries	Non PDS Beneficiaries	PDS Beneficiaries	Non PDS Beneficiaries		
1.	Illiterate	14	17	8	17	56	18.7
2.	Primary	44	40	31	40	155	51.7
3.	Secondary	17	18	28	18	81	27.0
4.	Above School level	—	—	8	—	8	26
	Total	75	75	75	75	300	100.00

Source: Computed from the primary data.

The Table 3.17 explains that out of 150 rural respondents, 10 PDS respondents and 3 non-PDS respondents are cultivators (Land holders), 36 PDS respondents and 23 non-PDS respondents are Agricultural labourers, 14 PDS respondents and 30 non-PDS respondents are non-Agricultural labourers, 7 PDS respondents, and 13 non-PDS respondents are doing business and 8 PDS respondents and 6 non-PDS respondents are working as professional. Out of 150 urban respondents, 7 PDS respondents and 4 non-PDS respondents are cultivators (land holders). 1 PDS respondents and 3 non-PDS respondent are Agricultural labourers, 49 PDS respondents and 53 non-PDS respondents are doing business and 11 PDS respondents and 3 non PDS respondents are working as professional.

To conclude, 146 respondents (48.7 percent) are working as non-Agricultural labourers, 63 respondent (21.0 per cent) are Agricultural laboures, 39 respondents (13.0 per cent) are doing business, 24 respondents (8.0 per cent) are cultivators (land holders) and 28 respondents (9.3 per cent) are working as professionals in Dindigul District. In the rural area, Agricultural labourers are higher than other labourers and in urban area, non-Agricultural labourers are higher. Thus, majority of sample respondents (48.7 per cent) is non-agricultural labour in Dindigul District.

Family size is also a deciding factor for food security because in a small family the access to food can be more and it may be positive. At a large, it cannot be denied that the family size is determined by certain sociological factors namely caste and religion and also the economic status has a role to play in determining the family size. Therefore the average family sizes in the rural and urban area under study is depicted in Table 3.18.

Table 3.17

Occupation—wise Classification of the Respondents

Sl. No.	Status	Rural		Urban		Total	Percentage
		PDS Beneficiaries	Non-PDS Beneficiaries	PDS Beneficiaries	Non PDS Beneficiaries		
1.	Cultivators	10	3	7	4	24	8.0
2.	Agri. labour	36	23	1	3	63	21.0
3.	Non-Agri. labour	14	30	49	53	146	48.7
4.	Business Man	7	13	7	12	39	13.0
5.	Profession	8	6	11	3	28	9.3
	Total	75	75	75	75	300	100.00

Source: Computed from the primary data.

Table 3.18

Average Family-size of the Sample Respondent

Sl. No.	Age	PDS Beneficiaries						Non PDS Beneficiaries					
		Rural			Urban			Rural			Urban		
		Male	Female	Total	Male	Female	Total	Male	Female	Total	Male	Female	Total
1.	0-15	48 (0.64)	22 (0.29)	70 (0.93)	56 (0.74)	53 (0.71)	109 (1.45)	28 (0.37)	15 (0.2)	43 (0.57)	41 (.55)	32 (0.42)	73 (0.97)
2.	16-35	30 (0.4)	94 (1.25)	124 (1.65)	76 (1.01)	69 (0.92)	145 (1.93)	46 (0.61)	32 (0.43)	98 (1.04)	29 (0.38)	58 (0.78)	87 (1.16)
3.	36-50	35 (0.46)	49 (0.65)	84 (1.11)	25 (0.33)	41 (0.55)	66 (0.88)	7 (0.09)	27 (0.36)	34 (0.45)	- -	22 (0.29)	22 (0.29)
4.	Above 50	19 (0.25)	23 (0.31)	42 (0.56)	2 (0.22)	16 (0.22)	18 (0.24)	5 (0.07)	11 (0.15)	16 (0.22)	2 (0.02)	11 (0.15)	13 (0.17)
	Average	1.75	2.5	4.25	2.1	2.4	4.5	1.14	1.14	2.28	0.95	1.64	2.59

Source: Computed from the primary data.

Note: Figures within parenthesis denotes average family size.

From the table 3.18, it is seen that the average family size of the PDS beneficiaries is 4.26 in rural areas and 4.5 in urban areas. But in the case of non-PDS beneficiary respondent, the average family size is very low, i.e., 2.54 in rural and 2.59 in urban areas. It is inferred that the family size influence, no doubt, the purchase of essential commodities from the ration shops.

The assets of the PDS and non-PDS respondent include the own house, land holdings, livestock and dead stocks like utensils, furniture, radio, cycle jewels, etc. The asset particulars of the sample respondents is exhibited in Table 3.19.

Table 3.19 reveals the average assets position of the PDS and non-PDS respondents in 1993-94 and in 1999-2000. It is clear that the total average assets value was increased from Rs. 21563 in 1993-94 to Rs. 35241 in 1999-2000. Nearly Rs. 14000 had increased during the study period. And the average assets value was increased from Rs. 91971 in 1993-94 to Rs. 115363 1999-2000, nearly Rs. 24000 had increased during the study period for the non-PDS beneficiaries.

Employment and Income

The categories of employment of the sample respondent are agriculture, non agriculture, business and government workers etc. The average annual employment of the PDS and non-PDS beneficiaries in the study district is presented in Table 3.20.

Table 3.20 explain the average annual employment level of the PDS and non-PDS respondents before 1993-94 and in 1999-2000. Rural areas constitute three villages namely, Perumal kovilpatti, Chinnalapatti and

Table 3.19

Average Asset--Level of Sample Respondent (Average value in Rs.)

Sl. No. Items	PDS Beneficiaries						
	1993-94			*1999-2000*			
	Rural	*Urban*	*Total Value*	*Rural*	*Urban*	*Total Value*	*Changes*
I. Land							
(*i*) Wet land	1130	1215	2345	1870	1650	3520	1175
(*ii*) Dry land	904	1050	1954	1010	1250	2260	306
2. Building	7014	22015	29029	9980	28340	38320	9291
3. Durables	2967	6427	9394	2893	10787	13680	4286
4. Livestock	3121	1820	4941	4616	2853	7469	2528
Total			21563			35249	13686

(*Table Contd...*)

Table (Contd...)

Sl. No.	Items	Non PDS Beneficiaries						
		1993-94			1999-2000			
		Rural	Urban	Total Value	Rural	Urban	Total Value	Changes
I.	Land							
	(i) Wet Land	1015	1450	2460	1200	1710	2910	450
	(ii) Dry land	675	1150	1825	850	1400	2250	425
	2. Building	22747	33815	56562	29871	34471	64342	8780
	3. Durables	9557	18987	28544	12848	28938	41786	13242
	4. Livestock	2079	501	2580	3210	865	4025	1495
	Total			97971			115363	23392

Source: Computed from the primary data.

Table 3.20

Average Annual Employment status of the sample respondent

(Average Number of Days)

Sl. No.	Occupation	PDS Beneficiaries		All	Non-Beneficiaries		All
		Rural	Urban		Rural	Urban	
I.	1993-94						
	1. Agri	314.4	35.04	349.44	485.04	19.20	504.24
	2. Non-Agri	218.88	188.16	407.04	166.08	363.84	529.92
	3. Profession	84.48	41.28	125.76	70.08	184.80	254.88
	4. Others	342.00	661.12	1003.12	122.40	393.00	515.40
	Total	959.76	925.60	1885.36	843.6	960.84	1804.44
II.	1999-2000						
	1. Agri	260.08	29.92	290.00	386.08	14.40	400.48
	2. Non-Agri	187.68	177.76	365.44	160.80	355.20	516.00
	3. Profession	92.47	44.15	136.62	242.88	496.80	739.68
	4. Others	463.68	646.08	1109.76	122.40	412.32	534.72
	Total	1003.91	897.91	1901.82	912.16	1278.72	2190.88

Source: Computed from the primary data

Note: Figures within parenthesis denoted average employment size by non PDS Beneficiaries.

Chettiyapatti. In Perumalkovilpatti village the respondents worked for 256 days per year in 1993-94 and 243 days in 1999-2000. The changes between these two years was nearly 13 days. In chinnalapatti village, the respondents worked for 304.8 days at an average level per year in 1993-94 and 264 days in 1999-2000 and nearly forty days decreased after implementation of New Economic Policy due to the unfavourable Government policy on textile industries at chinnalapatti.

The total number of working days of the PDS respondents on an average was 280.0 days per year before 1993-94. In Urban areas the total number of working days of the PDS respondents on an average was 313.8 days per year at present in urban areas. At present the total number of working days of the PDS respondents on an average are 250.4 days per year in rural area. In the urban area, the total number of working days of the PDS respondents on an average is 307.84 days per year. Thus, we conclude that the number of working days has reduced from 280 to 250.4 in rural areas, which is equal to 30.4 days. Similarly in urban area, the number of working days has reduced from 313.8 to 307.84 which is equal to 5.96 days.

Income is the deciding factor for one's standard of living, access to food, economic status, access to various infra-structural facilities, family size and type. Thus the monthly income of respondents analysed in Table 3.21 and 3.22.

Table 3.21 and 3.22 shows the average monthly income of the PDS and non PDS respondents before 1993-94 and in 1999-2000. Among the PDS Beneficiaries, a comparison between before 1993-94 and in 1999-2000 in

Table 3.21

Average Monthly Income of the PDS Respondents

(value in Rs.)

Area	PDS Beneficiaries										
	1993-94					1999-2000					
	Agri	Non-Agri	Profession	Others	Total	Agri	Non-Agri	Profession	Others	Total	Changes
I. Rural											
1. Perumal Koil patti	560	456.20	120	265.4	1401.6	640.4	634.8	200	358	1833.2	+431.6
2. Chinna lappatti	564	666	104.4	170	1504.4	714	716	112	220	1762	+257.6
3. Chettiyapatti yapatti	602	165	108	300	1176	736	284	120	360	1500	+324
Average	575.3	429.06	110.8	245.13	1306.6	696.8	544.9	144	312.6	1698.4	337.7
II. Urban											
1. Y.M.R. patti	650	738	160	1068	2616	1572	918	200	1714	4404	+1788
2. Balakrishnapuram	40	884	80	679	1680	80	1432	100	870	2482	+802
3. Trichy Road	240	1002	420	848	2510	360	1340	580	1460	3740	+1230
Average	310	874.6	220	865	2268.6	670.6	1230	303	1348	3542	1273.3

Source: Computed from the Primary data.

Table 3.22

Average Monthly Income of the Non-PDS Respondents

(value in Rs.)

Area	Non PDS Beneficiaries										
	1993-94					1999-2000					
	Agri	*Non Agri*	*Profession*	*Others*	*Total*	*Agri*	*Non-Agri*	*Profession*	*Others*	*Total*	*Changes*
I. Rural											
1. Perumal Koilpatti	594.2	329.2	56	907.4	1886.8	848.8	555.6	72	1282.4	2758.8	+872.0
2. Chinna lapatti	523.4	76	182	516	1297.4	665.6	161.6	218	703.6	1748.4	+451.0
3. Chetti yapati	666	124	314	832.4	2936.4	2496	164	828	1194.8	4682.8	+1746.0
Average	927.8	176.4	184	751.9	2040.2	1336.8	293.7	372.6	3180.8	3063.3	+10231
II. Urban											
1. YMR patti	952	1056	120	1666	3794	1004	1456	180	2500	5140	+1346.0
2. Balakrishnapuram	1374	140	929.24	2756.44	441.2	1732	184	1331.2	3688.4	931.96	+313.2
3. Trichy Road	120	284	–	708	1112	152	422.4	–	1040	1614.40	+502.4
Average	461.7	904.6	86.6	1101.08	2554.1	532.4	1203.4	121.3	1623.7	2480.9	+926.7

Source: Computed from the Primary data.

rural areas shows that PDS average income had increased from Rs. 2040.2 to Rs. 3063.3. A comparison of before 1993-94 and in 1999-2000 in urban areas the average income had increased from 2554.1 to 3480.8 by the non-PDS Beneficiaries.

The table 3.22 also reveals that the average income of rural non-PDS beneficiaries had increased from Rs. 2040.2 to Rs. 3063.3 i.e. nearly Rs. 1100 they are earning to meet the price rise in the Public Distribution System and the urban PDS Beneficiaries, average income had increased from Rs. 2554.2 to Rs. 3480.9 i.e., nearly Rs. 850 they are higherly earning from the urban sources.

Expenditure Pattern

The total annual consumption expenditure of the household classified as:

(i) Food Expenditure

(ii) Non-food Expenditure

Expenditure of food expenditure includes the expenditure on cereals, rice, wheat, sugar, rava, maida, palmolin oil, kerosene, pulses, fruits, edible oil, vegetables, milk and milk products, egg, fish and meat etc., Expenditure on non-food items refers to expenditure made by the households on education, entertainment, toilets, and cosmetics, newspaper and magazines, postage, charity gifts and donations, etc.

The consumption pattern of the PDS Beneficiaries and non-PDS Beneficiaries are analysed in this section. The expenditure items are classified into food items and non-food items. The consumption expenditure on food items by the PDS beneficiaries before 1993-94 and at present are compared in Table 3.24.

Table 3.23

Average Monthly Consumption Expenditure on food items by PDS Respondent

Sl. No.	Items	1993-94						1999-2000					
		Own		PDS		Open		Own		PDS		Open	
		Q	V	Q	V	Q	V	Q	V	Q	V	Q	V
1.	Rice	11.6	80	12.6	58.1	45.3	168.7	8.06	78.2	37.7	147.69	29.60	366.67
2.	Wheat	-	-	2.2	10.85	2.53	11.46	-	-	4.21	31.7	1.94	28.10
3.	Sugar	-	-	10.9	11.12	3.92	70.1	-	-	3.77	48.2	3.64	56.2
4.	Rava	-	-	1.1	3.98	0.9	6.3	-	-	0.59	6.12	1.22	13.75
5.	Maida	-	-	1.96	3.67	1.0	8.03	-	-	0.53	5.78	0.71	8.0
6.	Kerosene	-	-	8.9	19.0	24.2	8.21	-	-	1.9	71.3	22.54	69.65
7.	Palmolin	-	-	1.18	17.6	2.0	98.4	-	-	0.39	12.72	4.25	174.08
8.	Other Oil	-	-	0.83	3.32	1.48	48.88	-	-	-	-	1.25	63.98
9.	Milk	1.9	10.3	-	-	24.09	139.6	1.3	11.6	-	-	30.84	326.00
10.	Egg	-	-	-	-	18.4	20.6	-	-	-	-	22.04	40.5
11.	Mutton	-	-	-	-	3.69	208.5	-	-	-	-	3.58	369.1
12.	Vegetables	-	-	-	-	70.12	252.9	-	-	-	-	-	319.8
13.	Fruits	-	-	-		15.1	62.75	-	-	-	-	-	106.13
14.	Others	-	-	-	-	-	325.4	-	-	-	-	-	346.9

Source: Computed from the primary data.

Q: Quantity in kilogram, litre, numbers, etc.

V: Value in Rs.

Table 3.23 explains the average monthly consumption expenditure on food item by the PDS respondents. The average monthly consumption expenditure of rice quantity changed by 6.5 kg and the value increased to Rs. 148.06. The change in wheat quantity is 2.4 kg and value increased to Rs. 37.8 followed by sugar whose quantity 7.4 kg at the value of Rs. 23.2. It is compared with the 1993-94 and in 1999-2000, the changes are not higher in the average monthly consumption expenditure on the palmolin oil, mutton, vegetables and fruits and other remain are all medium level change.

Table 3.24 briefly explains the average monthly consumption expenditure on non-food items by PDS respondent. It is cleared that the changes on the non-food expenditure of the PDS beneficiaries was Rs. 2582.97 Among the various expenditures, the changes on cloth expenditure was higher than other expenditures. The changes was very meagre in the case of house rent item.

Average Monthly Consumption Expenditure by the Non-PDS Respondent

The average monthly consumption expenditure of non-PDS Beneficiaries are explained in Table 3.25. The table concludes that the expenditure on all food items except expenditure on egg have been increased due to the changes in the price level in open market. The egg price level is steady for past five years due to the mass production of eggs in Tamil Nadu. While comparing the consumption expenditure on food items for the different two periods (1993-94 and 1999-2000), the PDS Beneficiaries expenditure had increased at a low level. At the same time, the non PDS beneficiaries consumption expenditure on food items had increased at a high level.

Table 3.24

Average Monthly Consumption Expenditure on Non-Food Item (in Rs.) by PDS respondents

Sl. No.	*Items*	*PDS Beneficiaries*						
		1993-94			*1999-2000*			
		Rural	*Urban*	*Total*	*Rural*	*Urban*	*Total*	*Changes*
1.	House Rent	200	153.75	345.4	162.5	182.9	353.75	+8.35
2.	Education	178.1	309.5	487.6	269.2	484.7	753.9	+266.3
3.	Medical	137.08	165.6	302.68	168.4	227.19	387.59	+84.91
4.	Cloth (Annual)	2143.1	2625.7	4768.8	2654.3	3907.3	6561.6	+1792.8
5.	Entertainment	64.3	98.29	162.59	89.27	130	219.27	+56.68
6.	Lottery & Drinking	50	65	115	89.68	289.05	378.73	+263.73
7.	Others	154.5	190.5	345	224.6	231.6	456.2	+111.2

Source: Computed from the primary data.

Table 3.25
Average Monthly Consumption Expenditure on Food Items of the Non PDS Respondent

Sl. No.	Items	1993-94				1999-2000			
		Own		Open		Own		Open	
		Q	V	Q	V	Q.	V	Q	V
1.	Rice	11.26	78.8	48.5	41.7	11.9	129.0	68.1	747.15
2.	Wheat	–	–	5.59	39.5	–	–	7.08	103.64
3.	Sugar	–	–	4.7	49.17	–	–	2.80	98.1
4.	Rava	–	–	3.4	24.14	–	–	3.11	72.8
5.	Maida	–	–	1.6	36.3	–	–	2.0	53.29
6.	Kerosene	–	–	40.92	243.4	–	–	43.5	726.0
7.	Palmolin	–	–	2.9	91.1	–	–	3.28	123.18
8.	Other Oil	–	–	1.03	91.5	–	–	0.64	92.0
9.	Milk	4.69	29.5	35.21	214.1	3.4	34.2	45.18	214.1
10.	Egg	–	–	27.24	77.16	–	–	27.22	40.2
11.	Mutton	–	–	3.56	163.9	–	–	3.78	381.2
12.	Vegetable	–	–	–	302.3	–	–	–	325.8
13.	Fruits	–	–	–	87.03	–	–	–	100.92
14.	Others	–	–	–	387.6	–	–	–	473.1

Source: Computed from the primary data.

Q: Quantity, V: Value in (Rs.)

Table 3.26 explains the average monthly consumption expenditure on non-food items by the non-PDS Beneficiaries. The average House rent expenditure was increased from Rs. 413.3 in 1993-94 to Rs. 548.8 in 1999-2000 and the Education expenditure from Rs. 1139 to Rs. 1313.7 during the same period. But Medical expenditure was decreased from Rs. 2505.8 in 1993-94 to Rs. 1347.2 in 1999-2000. Table concludes that except Medical expenditure all other non-food expenditure by non-PDS beneficiaries have increased during the same period.

From the table 3.27 it is clear that average annual food expenditure on PDS beneficiary household is Rs. 11531.60 and non food expenditure is Rs. 11185.63 during the period 1993-94 and in 1999-2000, the average annual food expenditure is Rs. 17185.54 and non-food expenditure is Rs. 13678.67 by the PDS Beneficiaries. The average food expenditure is Rs. 13668.68 and Non-food expenditure is 13390.07 in 1993-94 and in 1999-2000. Annual food expenditure is 22434.97 and non-food expenditure is Rs. 25690.53 by the Non-PDS Beneficiaries. It is inferred that, nearly Rs. 8200 had increased from 1993-94 to 1999-2000 by PDS beneficiary and nearly Rs. 21066.75 had increased from 1993-94 to 1999-2000 by the non-PDS beneficiaries.

INCOME INEQUALITY

The level of money income of the individual households is closely related to the standard of living. The distribution of money among members of the community determines standards of living. In macro economic analysis, this must be taken into account because spending and saving habits are different at different income levels. So they gave consumers preferences and the distribution

Table 3.26

Average Monthly Consumption Expenditure on Non-food Items by Non-PDS Respondent

Sl. No.	Items	1993-94			1999-2000			
		Rural	*Urban*	*Total*	*Rural*	*Urban*	*Total*	*Changes*
1.	House Rent	233.3	180	413.3	325	223.8	548.8	135.5
2.	Education	820.1	318.9	1139	908.3	405.4	1313.7	174.7
3.	Medical	2112.7	393.1	2505.8	920.2	427	3147.2	1158.6
4.	Cloth	2687.3	2619.3	5306.6	3672.4	3060.8	6733.2	1426.6
5.	Entertainment	211.69	176.8	388.49	249.7	193.25	443.28	54.79
6.	Lottery & Drinking	1663	137.6	303.9	240.7	146.25	386.95	83.05
7.	Others	343.1	270.4	613.5	484.9	430.2	915.1	301.6

Source: computed from the primary data.

Table 3.27

Average annual consumption expenditure on food and non-food items

Sl. No.	*Items*	*1993-94* *Rs.*	*1999-2000* *Rs.*	*Changes* *Rs.*
1.	**PDS Beneficiaries**			
	(i) Food	11531.60	17185.54	5653.94
	(ii) Non-Food	11185.63	13678.67	2493.04
	Total	22717.23	30864.21	8146.98
2.	**Non-PDS Beneficiaries**			
	(i) Food	13668.68	22434.97	8766.29
	(ii) Non-food	13390.07	25690.53	12300.46
	Total	27058.75	48125.50	21066.75

Source: Computed from the primary data.

Table 3.28

Cumulative Percentage of Number of Households and Income of PDS Beneficiaries in 1993-94

Income Size	*No. of House holds*	*Amount of Household Income (in Rs.*	*Cumulative No. of House holds*	*Cumulative Amount of households (in Rs.)*	*Cumulative Percentage of households*	*Cumulative Percentage households income*
Below 25000	116	1772500	116	17722500	77.33	49.43
25001-45000	23	728400	139	2500900	92.66	69.75
45001-65000	5	268800	144	2769700	96.00	77.24
65001-85000	1	84000	145	2853700	96.66	79.59
85001-105000	2	188000	147	3041700	98.00	84.83
105001-and above	3	543800	150	3585500	100.00	100.00

Source: Computed from the primary data
Gini Ratio = 0.2

Table 3.29

Cumulative Percentage of Number of Households and Income of PDS Beneficiaries in 1999-2000

Income Size	*No. of Households*	*Amount of Household Income (in Rs.)*	*Cumulative No. of Households*	*Cumulative Amount of Households Income (in Rs.)*	*Cumulative percentage of of households*	*Cumulative percentage of of house hold Income*
Below 25000	79	12,85,520	79	12,85,520	52.66	26.73
25001-45000	50	15,35,700	129	28,21,220	86.00	58.67
45001-65000	5	2,85,000	134	31,06,220	89.33	64.60
65001-85000	8	5,82,500	142	36,88,720	94.66	76.71
85001-105000	2	1,73,500	144	38,62,220	96.00	80.32
105001-and above	6	9,46,000	150	48,08,220	100.00	100.00

Source: Computed from the primary data.

Gini Ratio = 0.35

Table 3.30

Cumulative Percentage of Number of Households and Income of Non PDS Beneficiaries in 1993-94

Income Size	*No. of House-holds*	*Amount of Household Income (in Rs.)*	*Cumulative No. of House-holds*	*Cumulative Amount of Households Income (in Rs.)*	*Cumulative Percentage of House-holds*	*Cumulative Percentage of House-holds Income*
Below 25000	107	15,43,692	107	15,43,692	71.33	36.33
25001-45000	19	6,18,700	126	21,62,392	84.00	50.90
45001-65000	9	48,68,800	135	26,49,192	90.00	62.36
65001-85000	2	1,72,850	137	28.22,042	91.33	66.43
85001-105000	8	7,29,350	145	35,51,392	96.66	83.59
105001-and above	5	6,96,700	150	42,48,092	100.00	100.00

Source: Computed from the primary data.
Gini Ratio = 0.40

Table 3.31

Cumulative Percentage of Number of Households and Income of Non-PDS Beneficiaries in 1999-2000

Income Size	*No. of House-Holds*	*Amount of Household Income (in Rs.)*	*Cummulative No. of House-holds*	*Cummulative Amount of Households Income*	*Cummulative percentage of House-holds*	*Cummulative percentage of House-holds Income*
Below 25000	76	12,98,810	76	12,98,810	50.66	20.97
25001-45000	42	13,47,240	118	26,46,050	78.66	42.73
45001-65000	6	3,35,060	124	29,81,110	82.66	48.14
65001-85000	5	3,96,400	129	33,50,510	86.00	54.11
85001-105000	8	7,54,800	137	41,05,310	91.33	66.30
105001-and above	13	20,86,000	150	61,91,340	100.00	100.00

Source: Computed from the primary data.

Gini Ratio = 0.43

of income governs the patterns of expenditure. It affects the level of aggregate personal savings. The income inequality has been analysed by using the formula for Gini Ratio.

$$\text{Gini Ratio (G)} = 1 - \frac{\sum_{K}^{N} (Pk - Pk\text{-}1)(Qk + Qk\text{-}1)}{10000}$$

P = Cumulative of Households

Q = Cumulative percentage of households

N = Number of classes used in this analysis.

If the concentration ratio is closer to zero, there is equal income distribution. If the ratio is not closer to zero, there is greater inequality of income distribution. Gini concentration ratio is calculated and tabulated beneficiary wise and it is shown in Table 3.32.

Table 3.32

Distribution of Gini Ratio

Sl. No.	*Beneficiaries*	*Gini ratio*
1.	PDS Beneficiaries in 1993-94	0.20
2.	PDS Beneficiaries in 1999-2000	0.35
3.	Non-PDS Beneficiaries in 1993-94	0.40
4.	Non-PDS Beneficiaries in 1999-2000	0.43

The above analysis reveals that the total annual gross income of the 150 PDS, 150 non-PDS sample house holds for the period of 1993-94 and 1999-2000 year in Dindigul District. Total household income is Rs. 35,85,500. The sources of income are classified into four categories, namely agricultural work, non-agricultural work, profession, others. The main source of their income households are classified into six groups on the basis of their annual gross income. The distribution of household income is analyzed with help of statical tools like average, percentage, and Gini coefficient. It implies that the households having high income are small in number and households having low income and large in number. However larger number of households is found in the income range of Rs. 25000-105001. The higher income groups are comparatively small in number but their influence on total income and expenditure is significant.

Savings and Indebtedness

Average monthly savings of the PDS and non-PDS beneficiary households are explained in Table 3.33. The sources of savings are Post Office, Banks, Private Money lenders and others. The table explains the saving amount comparison between the year 1993-94 and 1999-2000 in urban and in rural areas by the PDS and non-PDS respondents.

The study found that on an average monthly savings had increased from Rs. 495.6 in 1993-94 to Rs. 652.8 in 1998-99 in rural areas and from Rs. 176.4 to Rs. 270 in Urban areas during the same period. There has been an increase of Rs. 217.1 from the year 1993-94 to 1999-2000 in rural areas and an amount of Rs. 198.2 increased from the year 1993-94 to 1999-2000 in urban areas by the non-PDS respondent. It is inferred that the average savings had increased by Rs. 271.1 among the non-PDS Beneficiaries in Rural areas while comparing before 1993-

Table 3.33

Average Monthly Savings of the Beneficiary Household

Sl. No.	Sources	PDS beneficiary			Non PDS beneficiary		
		Rural	Urban	Total	Rural	Urban	Total
1993-94							
1.	Post office	206.1	71.3	277.4	258.4	92.6	351.5
2.	Bank	137.6	61.6	198.9	295.5	820.6	1116.1
3.	Private Money Lenders	88.3	38.1	126.4	134.9	259.6	394.5
4.	Others	63.8	5.3	69.1	20.6	17.8	38.4
	Total	495.5	176.3	671.8	709.9	1190.6	1900.5
1999-2000							
1.	Post office	330.5	112.7	443.2	387.1	127.3	514.4
2.	Bank	129.1	89.9	219.0	328.2	334.4	662.6
2.	Private Money Lenders	117.6	60.0	177.6	181.4	349.4	5308
3.	Others	75.5	7.3	82.8	30.4	30.7	61.1
	Total	652.7	269.9	922.6	927.1	841.8	1768.9
	Changes in Average Monthly Savings	157.2	93.6	250.8	217.2	348.8	131.6

Source: Computed from the Primary data.

94 and 1999-2000 and Rs. 157.2 had increased in rural areas among the PDS Beneficiaries.

The average annual indebtedness of the PDS and Non-PDS respondents are given in table 3.34. The study found that the changes in the average annual indebtedness of the PDS beneficiary households was Rs. 2397 in rural areas and Rs. 4174 in urban areas. The non PDS beneficiary household's average annual indebtedness had increased from Rs. 15188.9 to Rs. 69923.1 in 1999-2000 in rural areas. And the changes in the average annual indebtedness of the Non-PDS beneficiary households was Rs. 56056.5. It is clear that the debt position of the PDS beneficiaries and Non-PDS beneficiary households have declined during the study period.

AWARENESS ABOUT PDS

Distance Between Home and Ration Shops

The beneficiaries' opinions about the distance between home and ration shop are explained in Table 3.35. The actual distance classified into two: less than 2 km and more than 2 km.

Table 3.35 explains the distance between home and ration shop by the respondents. Of the 300 PDS and non PDS respondents in rural and urban, 105 PDS respondents and 103 non PDS respondents reveals that the distance between home and ration shop is less than 2 km and for 45 PDS respondents it is more than 2 km. The opinion about the ration shop is also explained in the same Table. Of the 300 PDS and non-PDS respondents, 78 PDS and 79 non-PDS respondents answered that the ration shop is convenient, 33 PDS respondent, 38 non PDS respondents asked to set up the ration shop in their nearby living areas.

Table 3.34

Average Annual Indebtedness of the Sample Respondents

Sl. No.	Sources	PDS Beneficiaries			Non-PDS Beneficiaries		
		Rural Rs.	Urban Rs.	Total Rs.	Rural Rs.	Urban Rs.	Total Rs.
1993-94							
1.	Bank	1426.6	5820	7246.6	6173.3	1373.3	7546.6
2.	Cooperative	640.0	790.6	1430.6	2244	493.3	2737.3
3.	Money Lenders	838.6	1764.0	2602.6	2884	4092	6976
4.	Friends and Relatives	712.0	2240.0	2952.0	4621.7	1420	6041.7
	Total	3617.2	10614.6	14231.8	15923	7378.6	23301.6
1999-2000							
1.	Bank	2300	9870	12170	7506.6	7580	15086.6
2.	Cooperative	940	1173.3	2113.3	3666.6	258.6	3925.2
3.	Money Lenders	1286.6	1273.3	2559.9	3555.3	2988	6541.3
4.	Friends and Relatives	238.6	1212.3	1665.2	2462.2	1453.3	3915.5
	Total	4765.2	13529.9	18508.4	17188.7	2279.9	29468.6
	Changes	1148	2915.3	4276.6	1265.7	4901.3	6167.0

Source: Computed from the primary data.

Table 3.35

Respondent Opinion about the Distance Between Home and Ration Shop

		PDS Beneficiaries			Non-PDS Beneficiaries				
S. No.	*Distance*	*Rural*	*Urban*	*Total*	*Rural*	*Urban*	*Total*	*Total*	*Percentage*
Actual									
1.	Below 2 km	68	37	105	38	63	101	206	68.66
2.	Above 2 km	7	38	45	37	12	49	94	31.34
	Total	75	75	150	75	75	150	300	100.00
Opinion									
1.	Convenient	40	38	78	44	35	79	157	52.33
2.	Inconvenient	12	21	33	15	23	38	71	23.67
3.	Setup Ration shop in their near by living areas	23	16	39	16	17	33	72	24.00
	Total	75	75	150	75	75	150	300	100.00

Source: Computed from the primary data.

Aware of Availability of Ration Items

The respondent response about the aware of availability of the ration items is explained in Table 3.36. The sources of awareness are Dhandora, Announcement, Notice Board, Friends and Relatives etc.

Table 3.36

Opinion about the Aware of Availability and Supply of the Ration Items by the PDS Beneficiaries

Sl. No.	*Source of Awareness*	*PDS Beneficiaries*			
		Rural	*Urban*	*Total*	*Percentage*
1.	Dhandora	6	3	9	6.0
2.	Announcement	5	41	46	30.66
3.	Notice Board	30	22	52	34.67
4.	Friends and Relatives	34	9	43	28.67
	Total	75	75	150	100.00

Source: Computed from the Primary data.

Table 3.36 reveals that most of the PDS beneficiaries came to know about the supply of PDS commodities in the concerned ration shops only through the notice board (34.67 per cent) and friends and relatives (28.67 per cent) in the study district.

Distributions of Ration Cards

The cardholders are receiving the card from the officials namely, Revenue official, village leaders and others. The details about the supply of ration cards to the beneficiaries are explained in Table 3.37.

Of the 190 cardholders, 115 cardholders have received the ration cards from the Revenue officials, 67

Table 3.37

Details about the Source of Receiving Ration Cards from the Officials

Sl. No.	Assistance	Rural	Urban	Total	Percentage
1.	Revenue Officials	72	43	115	60.53
2.	Village leaders	55	12	67	35.26
3.	Others	3	5	8	4.21
	Total	130	60	190	100.0

Source: Computed from the Primary data.

respondents have received the ration cards from the village leaders and 8 respondents have received the ration cards from the sources.. So, the revenue officials and village leaders play a significant role in the supply of ration cards to the beneficiaries of PDS.

Quality of the PDS Commodity

The PDS Beneficiary opinion about the quality of the PDS commodity are explained in Table 3.38. The selected PDS commodities are Rice, Wheat, Sugar, Rava, Maida, Kerosene, Palmolin oil, etc.

Table 3.38 shows the quality of PDS Commodities where 70 respondents of Rice buyer's opinion's is good. 63 respondent's opinion's is fair, and 17 respondent's opinion's is poor, 75 wheat purchaser's opinion's is good, 40 respondent's opinion is fair, and 35 respondent's opinion is fair. 43 sugar buyer's opinion is good, 68 respondent's opinion is poor and 39 respondent's opinion is poor, 57 Rava purchaser's opinion is good, 56 respondent's opinion is fair, 37 respondent's opinion is poor, 32 Maida purchaser's opinion is good, 61 respondent's opinion is fair, and 57 respondent's opinion is poor, 32 kerosene

Table 3.38

PDS Beneficiaries opinion about the quality of the PDS Commodities

Sl. No.	Items	PDS Beneficiaries								
		Rural			Urban			Total		
		Good	Fair	Poor	Good	Fair	Poor	Good	Fair	Poor
1.	Rice	25	38	12	45	25	5	70	63	17
2.	Wheat	36	22	17	39	18	18	75	40	35
3.	Sugar	19	36	10	24	32	19	43	68	39
4.	Rava	26	34	15	31	22	22	57	36	37
5.	Maida	12	32	31	20	29	26	32	61	57
6.	Kerosene	21	34	20	11	41	23	32	75	43
7.	Palmolin	10	47	18	20	49	6	30	96	24
	Total	149	273	123	190	216	119	339	439	252

Source: Computed from the primary data.

buyer's opinion is good, 75 respondent's opinion is fair, and 43 respondent's opinion is poor, and 30 palmolin oil buyer's opinion is good, 96 respondent opinion is fair, and 24 respondent's opinion is poor.

The table shows that a large number of respondent's opinions on rice and wheat quality are good, but the opinion on kerosene and palmolin is fair. The opinion about the quality of PDS Sugar, rava and maida is poor quality. As per the opinion of this study, the government may cut down the poor quality commodities and necessary steps would be taken to supply the best quality goods under PDS.

Quantity

Consumers benefit of public distribution system at aggregate level was obtained the tune of Rs. 18.36 crores for the year 1991-92. Sugar, wheat and rice contributed to Rs. 12.29 Rs. 4.26 and Rs. 1.41 crores respectively. In Fair Price Shop, all the commodities are underweight and it must be ensured to the people, especially below poverty line. The respondent opinion about the quantity of PDS Commodity are explained in Table 3.39.

Table 3.39 revealed the PDS Beneficiary opinion about the quantity of PDS Commodity in rural area and in urban area. Rice commodity supplied to the card holders is from 17 kg to 18 kg, but average requirements for one family is 50 kg. Wheat commodity supplied to the public is only 5 kg, which is not enough to a family. Sugar supplied 1.5 kg to 2 kg but an actual requirement is 3 kg. Rava and maida supplied is 1 kg only. Kerosene supplied under PDS is 2 litres per card but actual requirement is 5 litres, palmolin oil supply is one litre. But in rural area, the palmolin is not supplied to the cardholder. Rice, sugar,

Table 3.39

PDS Beneficiary Opinion about the Quantity of the PDS Commodity

RURAL								
Sl. No.	*Commodity*	*Quantity Fixed by Govt. per unit*	*Average Actual*	*Average Supply*	*Adequate*	*Inadequate*	*Total*	*Average of Actual requirement per unit*
1.	Rice	20	20	18	56	19	75	50
2.	Wheat	5	5	5	43	32	75	5
3.	Sugar	2	2	1.5	39	3	75	3
4.	Rava	2	2	1	62	13	75	3
5.	Maida	2	2	1	54	21	75	3
6.	Kerosene	3	3	2	27	48	75	2
7.	Palmoline oil	1	–	–	–	–	–	1

(Table Contd...)

(Table Contd...)

URBAN								
Sl. No.	*Commodity*	*Quantity Fixed by Govt. per unit*	*Average Actual*	*Supply*	*Adequate*	*Inadequate*	*Total*	*Average of Actual requirement per unit*
1.	Rice	20	20	175	56	19	75	70
2.	Wheat	5	5	5	49	26	75	5
3.	Sugar	2	2	2	52	23	75	3.5
4.	Rava	2	2	1.5	61	14	75	3
5.	Maida	2	2	1.5	45	30	75	1
6.	Kerosene	10.5	10.5	9.5	31	44	75	15.0
7.	Palmoline oil	1	1	1	43	32	75	1.5

Source: Computed from the primary data.

wheat, Rava, Maida are also adequate to the rural people but at same time, kerosene is not adequate to the most of the card holders family. Most of the respondents opinion is that they want more quantity of kerosene.

In urban areas, the supply of Rice commodity from 17 kg to 20 kg. But average actual requirements are 70 kg and it is not enough to the most of the cardholder, wheat and sugar supply are 5 kg and wheat requirement is enough. Kerosene supply is 10 litres in corporation areas, 5 litres in Municipality area. But actual requirement is 15 litres in the Corporation area and 8 litres in Municipality area.

It is inferred that the supply of Rice, Wheat, sugar, Rava, Maida and Palmolin under PDS are adequate to the family. But kerosene is not adequate to the PDS beneficiaries.

Legalization of Ration Card

Table 3.40 explains the legalization of PDS cards given to others by the respondents. Of the 150 PDS respondents, 119 PDS respondents are aware that about the card given to others is legally wrong. But 31 PDS respondents are not awareness about the card given to others that is legally wrong. Of the 150 non-PDS beneficiary, 122 respondents are aware and 28 respondents are not aware about the cards given to others.

It is clear that 40.66 percent of non-PDS respondents and 39.66 PDS respondents are aware about the cards given to others as legally wrong.

ATTITUDES AND PRACTICE BY RESPONDENT ON PDS

The attitude of the PDS beneficiaries and non-PDS beneficiaries towards the purchase/produce on their own. PDS, open market are explained in Table 3.41. The essential commodities are rice, wheat, sugar, rava, maida, kerosene and palmolin oil etc.

Table 3.40

Respondents Awareness about Legalization of Card Given to Others

Sl. No.	*Area*	*Awareness of Legalization*						*Total*
		PDS Beneficiaries			*Non PDS Beneficiaries*			
		Yes	*No*	*Total*	*Yes*	*No*	*Total*	
1.	Rural							
	(*a*) Card holder	50	15	65	28	3	31	96
	(*b*) Non-card holder	8	2	10	35	9	44	54
2.	Urban							
	(*a*) Card holder	55	10	65	21	8	29	94
	(*b*) Non-card holder	6	4	10	38	8	46	56
	Total	119	37	150	122	28	150	300

Source: Computed from the Primary data.

Table 3.41

Details about the Commodities Purchased by the PDS Beneficiaries

Sl. No.	Commodities	No. of PDS Beneficiaries					
		Open	Own	PDS	Own & PDS	PDS & Open	Own PDS & Open
1.	Rice	20 (13.4)	16 (10.6)	90 (60.0)	11 (7.4)	13 (8.6)	—
2.	Wheat	—	—	128 (85.4)	—	5 (3.3)	—
3.	Sugar	—	5 (3.3)	133 (88.7)	4 (2.7)	8 (5.3)	—
4.	Rava	—	—	21 (85)	—	3 (15)	—
5.	Maida	—	—	24 (80)	—	6 (20)	—
6.	Kerosene	—	—	143 (95.4)	—	7 (4.6)	—
7.	Palmolin Oil	59 (39.3)	6 (4)	62 (41.3)	—	23 (15.4)	—

Source: Computed from the primary data.

Note: Figures within the Parenthesis denotes percentages

Regarding the purchase of rice, 90 PDS beneficiary respondent (60.0 per cent) purchase the rice only from PDS ration shops and also 20 sample respondents (13.4 per cent) purchase the rice from the open market only. The study found that a large number of respondents are using the PDS benefits for all essential commodities.

Table 3.42

Responses on the Reasons for not Receiving the Ration Commodity by the Card Holder

Sl. No.	*Reasons*	*Rural*		*Urban*		*Total*	
		Yes	*No*	*Yes*	*No*	*Yes*	*No*
1.	Shortage of Weight	12	19	10	19	22	38
2.	Inadequate allotted Quota	8	23	7	22	15	45
3.	Non-availability of Ration items	16	15	6	23	22	38
4.	Long Distance	14	17	5	24	19	41
5.	Ration shop not function regularly	5	26	10	19	15	45
6.	Not suitable time for purchasing period	20	11	13	16	33	27
7.	Status problem	5	26	8	21	13	47
8.	Quality not good	10	21	8	21	18	42
9.	Own commodity	9	22	1	28	10	50
10.	Mortgage of ration Card	1	30	7	22	8	52
11	Ration commodity Price is high	9	22	6	23	15	45
12.	Money problem	8	23	9	20	17	43

Source: Computed from the primary data.

Table 3.42 explains the reasons for not receiving the PDS commodity by the cardholders of Non-PDS beneficiary. In rural area, most of the cardholders revealed that the time for purchasing is not suitable and shortages of weight and non-availability of ration items at the required time.

In urban area also, the reasons for not purchasing the ration items are: no suitable time for purchasing, shortages at weight, ration shop not functioning regularly in study district. Of the 60 cardholders of non-PDS respondents, 33 cardholders stated that no suitable time for purchasing and 8 respondents answered that the card is mortgaged due to lack of money.

The reasons for not receiving Ration card from the office by the Non-PDS respondent are explained in Table 3.43. The reasons are classified into six i.e., not necessary, change of native place, recently applied, card cancelled, already applied but delay in supply of card and not applied.

Table 3.43

Responses on Reasons for not Receiving the Card by non-card Holders

Sl. No.	*Reasons*	*Rural*	*Urban*	*Total*	*Percentage*
1.	Not Necessary	7	11	18	16.36
2.	Change of Native Place	4	6	10	9.09
3.	Recently applied	16	21	37	33.64
4.	Card cancelled	6	10	16	14.55
5.	Already applied but delay in supply of card	8	4	12	10.90
6.	Not applied	7	10	17	15.46
	Total	48	62	110	(100.00)

Source: Computed from the primary data.

Table 3.44

Respondents opinion about the other uses of Ration Card

Sl. No.	Other Uses	Rural			Urban			Total		
		Yes	No	Total	Yes	No	Total	Yes	No	Total
1.	School Admission	15	34	49	22	28	50	37	62	99 (33.0)
2.	License/passport	24	26	50	40	30	70	64	56	120 (40.00)
3.	Family Identification	36	15	51	13	17	30	49	32	81 (27.0)
	Total	75	75	150	75	75	150	150	150	300 (100.00)

Source: Computed from the primary data.

Note: Figures within parenthesis denotes percentage.

The study found that most of the non-cardholders applying recently for the ration card to the taluk office in the study district.

The awareness about the other uses of ration cards are given in Table 3.44. The ration card has a number of uses besides buying commodities from PDS shops. The other uses of ration card are school admission, license and passport and family identification. The 40.0 per cent of respondent revealed that the ration card is used for getting a license and passport by the cardholder and non-cardholders.

The PDS System is to function in a good way but due to some problems it is not able to do so. The respondent opinion about the way of good functioning fair price shops are exhibited in Table 3.45. The suggestions are: functioning regularly (21 per cent), supply entitled quota of ration (25.66 per cent), Display the availability of ration everyday (13.34 per cent) and weightment must be ensured (40.0 per cent). It is inferred that supply of PDS commodities at correct weight would pave the way for effective functioning of PDS in Dindigul district of Tamil Nadu.

The PDS Schemes is especially benefits the rural people and the government is to depute the management of PDS to the gram panchayat. The respondent opinion about the Gram Panchayat run by the PDS is explained in Table 3.46.

The Table 3.46 explains the respondent opinion about running of PDS by the Gram Panchayat. Majority of the respondents (71.34 per cent) had accepted the running of PDS effectively by the Gram Panchayat or under New Panchayat Raj System.

Table 3.45

Respondent Suggestion for effective functioning of Fair Price Shop

Sl. No.	*Ways*	*Rural*	*Urban*	*Total*	*Percentage*
1.	Functioning regularly	21	42	63	21.00
2.	Supply entitled Quota of ration	54	23	77	25.66
3.	Display the availablity	26	14	40	13.34
4.	Weightment must be ensured	49	71	120	40.0
	Total	150	150	300	100.00

Source: Computed from the primary data.

Table 3.46

Respondent Opinion about the Involvement of Gram Panchayat to Run the Fair Price Shop

Sl. No.	*Opinion*	*Rural*	*Urban*	*Total*	*Percentage*
1.	Yes	90	124	214	71.34
2.	No	60	26	86	28.66
	Total	150	150	300	100.00

Source: Computed from the primary data.

The above analyses on the functioning of Public Distribution System during the deregulation period in Dindigul District of Tamil Nadu give clear cut picture about the changes in the social, economic and cultural attitudes of the people after implementation of New Economic Policy. The income and employment pattern, consumption pattern, savings and indebtedness level of the PDS beneficiaries and non-PDS beneficiaries have also changed with the influence of the deregulation under economic reforms in our country.

4

Summary and Conclusion

A summary of the study is presented in this chapter. The summary of the findings is detailed in the first section of this chapter. The second section reviews some problems in the implementation of Public Distribution System after the introduction of New Economic Policy in Tamil Nadu. The last section presents recommendation of few suggestions for the effective functioning of the PDS during the liberalisation period.

Summary of The Findings

Introduced in response to very critical food shortages in the 1960's, PDS has evolved into a price support-cum-subsidy program. The program has continued more or less unchanged although the food scenario at the macro (national) level has changed from one of scarcity to a surplus situation. PDS subsidies account for substantial budgetary expenditures at the central level; public spending levels are exceptionally high in which have there own subsidy programs. Moreover, the country is implementing an economic reform program. At no time is the question of the efficacy of PDS as a safety net more relevant than now, especially since the Government has recently embarked on drastic reforms of the system. Although PDS is an over researched subject in India, few studies have analyzed subsidy of PDS and government intervention and costs of PDS relative to other similar programs. Almost no studies exist that compare welfare and costs of the PDS beneficiaries and non-beneficiaries. This study aim was to fill this gap.

In order to evaluate the impact of food distribution policy on economic redistribution we have to look at prices, income and profits. In order to study the impact of the policy on prices, one needs to have a long term perspective. The PDS has contributed significantly to price stabilization and hence, stabilization and protection of entitlement. In period of severe droughts, the government releases additional amounts of foodgrains through the PDS. The result has been stabilization of supply, prices and quantities consumed. Public distribution System is now "Perceived" to the main safety net to protect the poor from potential short-run price induced adverse effects on the economic reforms currently under way, but the perception appears to be far from reality. The specific objectives of the study are: (i) To find out the rate of reduction in subsidies for supplies through PDS and its effect on PDS prices; (ii) To analyse the impact of the price and quantity changes for PDS Commodities on pattern of total expenditure, consumption, savings of the PDS Beneficiaries; (iii) To make a comparative study of PDS prices and the open market prices for the commodities distributed under PDS so as to estimate implicit subsidy borne by the society.

The primary data as well as secondary data were used for the present study. In order to analyze the functions and performance of Public Distribution System in Dindigul District, data for 10 years from 1986-87 to 1995-96 were collected from the Department of Civil Supplies. The budget allocation, subsidy rate, expenditure for PDS, price variation, quantities supplied etc. were analyzed with the help of secondary data. For collection of secondary data various sources were tapped. The predominant among them were Directorate of Food and Supplies, Government of Tamil Nadu, Ministry of Food, Government of India, Economic and Statistical Advisor to the Government of India, Ministry of Finance and District Food and Supplies Controller, Dindigul. Data on production, procurement and distribution of wheat and rice were taken for various issues of Bulletin of Food Statistics.

For the micro level analysis Dindigul District was purposively selected for the study because the researcher is familiar with the District. One taluk for the district was selected on the basis of the larger number of PDS beneficiaries. After selecting sample taluk for the study, one town and one panchayat in the taluks were selected on the basis of the same criterion.

A sample of 75 PDS Beneficiaries and 75 non-beneficiaries of PDS from the sample town and sample panchayat were randomly selected with the help of ration cards. A total of 150 PDS and 150 non-PDS Beneficiaries were interviewed with the pre-tested questionnaire. The primary data were collected from ration cardholders and non-card holders through interview using well structured, pre-tested interviewed schedule. Separate interview schedule was used for each respondent of PDS and non-PDS beneficiaries. The primary data on various aspects were collected during the year 1999-2000.

Simple average and tabular analysis was used to analyse the secondary and primary data. Other suitable statistical techniques were also used in the study. Before and after technique and comparative analysis were used in order to study the impact of the economic reform of a PDS in Tamil Nadu. The reference year was 1993-94 because in the year Government of Tamil Nadu introduced changes in the PDS in response to the economic reform.

THE MAIN FINDINGS OF THE STUDY ARE SUMMARISED BELOW

After 1992-93, the economy has picked up and the growth rate had reached an average level of 7 per cent during the period of 3 years (1994-95 to 1996-97). This can be considered as a legitimate achievement of the economic reforms.

Regarding the annual allocation of rice, it has continuously increased from 11.36 million tonnes in 1992 to 13.32 million tonnes in 1994-95. The increasing procurement and the declining off-take have caused stocks of foodgrains at FCI godowns reached unmanageable levels.

Periodic central issue prices of fine rice are increased from Rs. 349 per tonne in 1990 to Rs. 617 per tonne in 1994. The rising issue prices have helped to keep the open market prices above levels that the market would have determined. The central government issue price is Rs. 375 per quintal in 1998-99. But the state government issue price has doubled as Rs. 700 per quintal in the same period.

The foodgrain supplies was increased from 8.0 million tonnes in 1991 to 17.4 million tonnes in 1999. The supply of foodgrains continuously increased and the Government of India was fully involved systematically in the supply of foodgrains to the cardholders. Total supply of foodgrains has been increased from 7.69 million tonnes in 1971 to 20.5 million tonnes in 1997.

The expenditure on central subsidy had declined by 27 per cent between 1992-93 and 1994-95. The distribution of the central subsidy for wheat and rice was more or less equal except in the year 1994-95, when the share of wheat has increased to 65 per cent. The rate of growth of central government expenditure on food subsidy slowed down after 1993-94. The cost of food subsidy increased from Rs. 63.90 crores to Rs. 1000 crores in the period from 1984-85 to 1998-99 in Tamil Nadu. The amount of subsidy had increased according to the growth of PDS beneficiaries in Tamil Nadu.

A higher procurement of paddy was handled only in Thanjavur district and Tiruvarur district of Tamil Nadu. Nearly, 3,10,000 million tonnes in Tanjavur and 3,00,000 million tonnes of paddy in Tiruvarur district were procured during the study period.

The number of fair price shops had increased from 23,125 in 1996 to 26,515 in 1999, as per the policy of the government to start at least one fair price shop in each revenue village.

The scale of supply of rice is 20 kgs for a period of one month per cardholder. The kerosene supply has allotted to the cardholders through the number of LPG connection. The cardholder having single LPG connection and the kerosene supply is 15 litres in the municipalities, 10 litres in the township and 3 litres in the rural areas in Tamil Nadu. The Kerosene bunks have opened for the supply of correct scale of supply to the cardholder and 362 kerosene bunks were functioned in the year 1999-2000.

There is no change in the limits of supply of PDS commodities to the cardholders for the years 1986-87 and 1995-96 in Dindigul District. Except wheat, limits of supply all the other was same, and the kerosene limit was increased from 5 litres to 10 litres in corporation areas.

After implementation of New Economic policy, the price of wheat had increased from Rs. 2.60 in 1991-92 to Rs. 4.50 in 1996-97 and the price of sugar had also increased from Rs. 5.25 to Rs. 9.05 during the same period. The essential commodities of Rice, Sugar, and Kerosene at PDS price level were lower than the open market prices. The price of wheat was Rs. 9.75, Rava was Rs. 12.80 and maida was Rs. 12.30 in the year 1999-2000.

The study observed that there is highly positive correlation between PDS price and open market prices of fine rice, wheat, sugar and palmolin oil, since it is significant at 1 per cent and 5 per cent level. The result of the t' test does not support the hypothesis that the variables in the price are highly correlated.

The rice stock had increased from 10110.118 tonne kilograms in 1986-87 to 13782.951 tonne kilograms in 1995-96. The wheat stock had also increased from 38.125 tonne kilograms to 399.589 tonne kilograms, during the same period. It is inferred that due to price revision and some other reasons, the stock of essential commodities had increased after implementation of New Economic policy.

In Dindigul District, rice supplies had increased from 34311.102 tonne kilograms in 1986-87 to 51226.986 tonne kilograms in 1995-96. Similarly, the supply of Sugar, Rava, Kerosene had also increased during the same period. Except wheat and palmolin oil, supplies of all other essential commodities are increased under PDS in Dindigul District.

The total number of ration shops had increased from 440 in 1986-87 to 558 in 1995-96 in Dindigul District. After implementation of New Economic Policy, it has risen from 492 in 1991-92 to 558 ration shops in 1995-96. A large number of ration shops is located in Dindigul Town Frika (Urban) and Chinnalapatti Frika (Rural).

The study found that a large number of ration cards were in circulation in Dindigul Town Frika (Urban) (39500) and Chinnalapatty Frika (Rural) (15400) in the year 1995-96 in Dindigul Taluk. The range number ration users are living in Dindigul Town Frika (Urban) and Chinnalapatti Frika (Rural) in Dindigul Taluk of Dindigul District.

Of the total PDS beneficiaries sample respondents, the 130 respondents are cardholders and 20 respondents are non-card holders and of the non-PDS beneficiaries 90 respondents are non card holders and 60 respondents are cardholders. It is inferred that 43.4 per cent of PDS beneficiaries are cardholders and 30.0 per cent of non-PDS beneficiaries are non-card holders.

Of the total sample respondents, 146 respondents (48.7 per cent) are working as non-agricultural labourers, 63 respondents (21.0 per cent) are agricultural labours, 39 respondents (13.0 per cent) are doing business, 24 respondents (8.0 per cent) are cultivators (land holders) and 28 respondents (9.3 per cent) are working as profession in Dindigul district. Thus, majority of sample respondents (48.7 per cent) is non-agricultural labour in Dindigul District.

The average family size of the PDS beneficiaries is 4.26 in rural areas and 4.5 in urban areas. But in the case of non-PDS beneficiaries respondent, the average family size is very low, i.e., 2.54 in rural and 2.59 in urban areas. It is inferred that the family size influence, no doubt, the purchase of essential commodities from the ration shops. The number of working days had reduced from 280.8 per year in 1994-95 to 250.4 per year in 1998-99 in rural areas, which is equal to 30.4 days. Similarly, in urban area, the number of working days had reduced from 313.8 per year to 307.84 per year, which is equal to 5.96 days, due to the natural calamities.

The study found that the large number of households is found in the income range of Rs. 25000-105001 in the study area. The higher income groups are comparatively small in number but their influence on total income and expenditure is significant. The average income of rural non-PDS beneficiaries had increased from Rs. 2040.2 to Rs. 3063. They are earning nearly Rs. 1100 additionally to meet the price rise in the Public Distribution System. The average income of the Urban PDS beneficiaries had increased from Rs. 2554.2 to Rs. 3480.9. They are earning nearly Rs. 850 additionally from the urban sources.

The PDS beneficiaries consumption expenditure was increased nearly Rs. 8200 and it was increased as Rs. 21066.75 to the non-PDS beneficiaries during the study period. After implementation of New Economic Policy, the changes in the average monthly food consumption expenditure on rice was 6.5 kg at the value of Rs. 148.06 and changes in wheat was 2.40 kg at the value of Rs. 37.80.

While, comparing the consumption expenditure on food items for the different two periods (1993-94 and 1999-2000) by PDS beneficiaries and non-PDS beneficiaries, the PDS beneficiaries expenditure had increased at a low level and the non-PDS beneficiaries consumption expenditure on food items had increased at a high level.

The change on the average annual non-food expenditure of the PDS beneficiaries was Rs. 2493.04. Among the various expenditures, the changes on cloth expenditure was higher than other expenditures. The changes were very meager in the case of house rent item. The average house rent expenditure was increased from Rs. 413.3 in 1993-94 to Rs. 548.8 in 1999-2000 and the education expenditure was increased from Rs. 1139 to Rs. 1313.7 during the same period.

On an average monthly saving of Rs. 271 had increased for the non-PDS beneficiaries and Rs. 157.2 for the PDS beneficiaries in rural areas, due to the low level of number of working days. The average debt position of the PDS beneficiaries and non-PDS beneficiaries households have declined during the study period.

45 PDS respondents revealed that the distance between home and ration shop is less than 2 km and it is more than 2 km for 78 PDS non-PDS respondents focused that the ration shop is convenient, 33 PDS and 38 non-PDS respondents suggested to setup the ration shop in their nearby living areas.

Most of the PDS beneficiaries came to know the supply of PDS commodities in the concerned ration shops through the notice board and friends (34.67 per cent) and through relatives (28.67 per cent) in the study district.

115 cardholders (60.53 per cent) have received the ration card from the revenue officials and 67 respondents (35.26 per cent) have received the ration cards from the village leaders.

A large number of respondents answered that rice and wheat qualities supplied through PDS are good, but the opinion on the quality of kerosene and palmoline oil is fair and poor quality of sugar, rava, and maida.

Most of the respondents revealed that the supply of Rice, Wheat, Sugar, Rava, Maida, Palmolin under PDS are adequate to the family, but the kerosene is not adequate to the PDS beneficiaries.

The reasons for not purchasing the ration items are: no suitable time for purchase; shortages of weight and irregular functioning of ration shops in study district. 8 respondents answered that the card is mortgaged due to lack of money.

The study found that most of the non-cardholders are applying recently (33.64) for the ration card to the taluk office in the study district.

The suggestion of the respondents for good functioning fair price shops are: functioning regularly (21 per cent), supply entitled quota of ration (25.66 per cent), display the availability of ration everyday (13.34 per cent) and ensuring correct weight (40.0 per cent). The study suggested that supply of PDS commodities at correct weightment would pave the way for effective functioning of PDS in Dindigul district of Tamil Nadu.

The respondent's opinion about running of PDS by the Gram Panchayat that majority of the respondents (71.34 per cent) had running of PDS effectively by the gram panchayat or under New Panchayat Raj System.

General Problem

During the last decades, the PDS dealt with between 11 and 19 tonnes per year, which is about 10 to 15 per cent of the total production of foodgrains in areas with surplus production, and distributes them in the whole country.

The quite sometime, the PDS was seen as an essential empowerment of India's food security policy. However, in the wake of the structural adjustment programme which was introduced in 1991, the PDS has been increasingly criticised.

In an attempt in bring down the subsidy, the Government of India has raised the PDS retail prices several time in the first half of the 1990's. It means that the price difference between PDS foodgrains and open market foodgrains come down and that the willingness of consumers to buy PDS commodities decreased. Subsequently, since procurement continues the result was an unprecedented high stock level.

In early 1999, a further price rise of Above Poverty Line (APL) foodgrains was introduced in order to reduce the subsidy for APL families. The policy is that Below Poverty Line (BPL) families receive 10 kilos of foodgrains per month at subsidised prices, While APL families receive a variable quantity for a higher price and only during a transition period.

FCI's total procurement and distribution costs (including processing, storage, and transport and packaging costs) have been increasing over the years and these costs have to be reimbursed as subsidy to the FCI. FCI's unit costs of operations have been increasing at a higher rate than that of the wholesale price Index for all commodities.

Regarding malnutrition, despite the huge subsidy and the large-scale of this PDS intervention, the food security of many vulnerable households is still marginal or insufficient. Distribution to the states has not been proportionate to the number of poor people in each state and within states the available supplies have not gravitated in favour of the poor.

Ration cards are issued only to those households who have proper registered residential addresses. This means that many of the poor who are homeless are left out.

The Public Distribution System has remained limited mostly to urban areas for a considerable period of planning while the coverage of rural areas was very insufficiency. While more than 75 per cent of the fair price shops are in rural areas, the level of their effectiveness in actual supply of essential commodities, particularly in rural, backward, remote and inaccessible areas were very limited.

At present, there is no uniform criterion in storage and issues of stock from the Food Corporation of India depots. Construction of godowns without much planning and consideration of release has resulted over the years in a situation where bigger godowns continues to be under utilised and smaller godowns over utilised.

Policy Implications

1. Keeping in view the twin objectives of economic development with social justice, the food subsidy may be continued in the near future. However, it may be restricted to the vulnerable population only.

2. Entitlement of commodities to be supplied through public distribution system in the state may be increased at least to the extent of minimum calorie requirement as per

recommendations of Indian Council of Medical Research.

3. For bringing efficiency in the system.
   (*a*) Commodities may be supplied at door-steps of fair price shops.
   (*b*) Fair price shops may be allotted to the residents of the same village in rural areas and that of the same locality and ladies may be given preference for allotment of such shops.
   (*c*) Efforts may be made to make fair price shop business remunerative, which could be done partly by increasing the number of ration cards per shop and partly by raising the rate of commission.
   (*d*) Efforts may be made to bring regularity in supply of PDS commodities.
   (*e*) The ration cardholders may be made aware of functions and composition of vigilance committees and formation of such committees may be taken up seriously.
4. In addition to terms of trade between monetary benefits and costs associated with PDS, while making policy decisions its indirect benefits may also be taken into consideration.
5. Display boards may be put up properly about the availability of stocks and availed number of cards in PDS Beneficiaries.
6. Distribution kerosene may be systematized as per the allotment and Gram panchayat may monitor the distribution regularly.

7. Panchayat Surpanch and revenue official may ensure that the genuine persons to get ration cards while recommending and duplicity of the family members may be avoided.

8. It is suggested that for smooth functioning of PDS, FCI should have storage capacity to maintain 3 months of stock to avoid delay in delivery of PDS articles. This means creation of adequate infrastructure and more investment of FCI.

9. This problem could be minimized if the state government takes of local procurement. The main problem of FCI is to deliver in right time and irregularity in transportation.

10. There is a need to reduce the number of PDS dealers and to introduce a system of composite dealership to serve better effective supervision and viable delivery. Steps should be taken to reduce the number of storage agents and retailers for a close and proper monitoring. Composite retailers should be appointed so that consumer gets all PDS commodities at a single place location.

11. If margin given to FPS Owners, there is a need to enhance the amount. The transport charges paid to storage agents and to the retailers should be enhanced. Moreover, Gram Panchayats as retailers, they should have some credit facility to lift the stock.

Conclusion

While concluding, the measures like composite dealership; doorstep delivery and enhancement of transport commission will improve the condition of PDS delivery at the cutting edge level. Along with that monitoring, vigilance, information about entitlement and accessibility factors form consumers point of view should be strengthened to improve the reach of the delivery of essential commodities. In order to avoid the transport and storage cost, the food stamps may be issued to the eligible households and they may be instructed to get the essential commodities from the open market by using the food stamps. The open market dealers may get the subsidy from the government by reimbursing the same food stamps.

Bibliography

Books

1. U.K. Singh, *"Public Distribution System"*, Mittal Publications, New Delhi, 1991. p. 134.

2. K.R. Venugopal, *"Deliverance from hunger the Public Distribution System in India"*, Sage Publications, New Delhi, 1992. p. 223.

3. B.N.P. Singh, *"Economic Liberalisation in India"*, Ashish Publishing House, New Delhi, 1994.

4. K.R. Gupta, *"Liberalisation and Globalisation of Indian Economy"*, Atlantic Publisher & Distributors, Vol. I, II, III, New Delhi, 1995.

5. B.P. Gupta, *"Challenges of Economics Reforms—Impact on labour and Industrial Relation"*, B.R. Publishing Cooperation, Delhi, 110052.

6. P.D. Hojela, *"Labour Restricting in India—A critique of the New Economic Policies"*, Communicators Publishers, New Delhi, 1998.

7. Jagdish Bhagwati, *"Food Aid Agricultural Production, and Welfare, Essay on Economic Progress and Welfare"*, Oxford University Press, Delhi, 1986. pp. 159-172.

8. M.L. Dantwala, *"The Food Problem and the Green Revolution Indian Economy"*, S. Chand & Company Ltd., New Delhi, 1995, pp. 499-514.

9. R. Radhakrishnan and Ravi, *"Food Demand in India Emerging Trends and Perspectives Studies in Indian Economy"*, Himalaya Publishing House, Delhi, 1996. pp. 403-436.

10. S.K. Misra, and V.K. Puri, *"Food Problem, Food Policy and Public Distribution System"*, Himalaya Publishing House, Delhi, June 1996, pp. 563-576.

11. T.N. Krishnan, *"The Marketed Surplus of Foodgrains Readings in Indian Agricultural Development"*, George Allen & Unwin Ltd., London 1972, pp. 99-109.

12. Raj Krishna, *"Government Operation in Foodgrains, Readings in Indian Agricultural Development"*, George Allen & Unwin Ltd, London, 1972, pp. 110-128.

13. R.C. Choudhry & Rajakutty (Ed), *Fifty Years of Rural Development in India: Retrospect and Prospect''*, NIRD Hyderabad, July 1998.

14. Rao, Linneman, *"Economic Reforms and Poverty Alleviation in India"*, Sage Publications, New Delhi, 1996.

15. N. Sivanna, *"Food Security and Panchayat Raj"*, Concept Publishing Company, New Delhi, 1997.

16. B.A. Prakash, *"Poverty, Food in take and PDS in Kerala: Kerala's Economic Development"*, Sage Publications, New Delhi, 1999.

17. K.K. Taimni, *"Studies in Retailing Consumer Cooperation and Public Distribution System"*, Harshad Prakashan Publishers, Poona, 1975.

18. Gilbert Etienme, *"Food and Poverty—India's Half Won Bathe"*, Sage Publications, New Delhi, 1988.

19. C.H. Hanumantha Rao Hans lineman, *"Economic Reforms and Poverty Alleviation in India"*, Sage Publications, New Delhi, 1996.

20. N. Krishnanji, T.N. Krishnan, *"Public Support for Food Security"*, Sage Publications, New Delhi, 1999.

21. D.S. Tyagi, *"Managing Indias Food Economy"*, Sage Publications, New Delhi, 1990.

22. Dy. Tyagi, Vijay Shakar Vyas, *"Increasing Access to Food"*, Sage Publication, New Delhi, 1990.

23. Mishra, Bhasshal, *"Economics of PDS in Foodgrains"*, Asia Publication House, New Delh, 1985.

24. S. Narayanan, *"Demand supply Gap and Public Distribution of Foodgrains in India"*, Aglicol Publishing Academy, New Delhi, 1986.

25. V.K. Sing, *"Public Distribution System"*, Mittal Publications, New Delhi, 1991.

26. K.C.S. Acharya, *"Food Security in India"*, Concept Publishing Limited, New Delhi, 1983.

27. R.N. Chopra, *"Evolution of Food Policy in India"*, Macmillian India Limited, New Delhi, 1981.

28. A.M. Khusto, *"Buffer Stocks and Storage of Foodgrains in India"*, Tata MC Graw Hill Publishing Co. Ltd., Bombay, 1973.

29. S.C. Joseph, *"Food Policy and Economic Development in India"*, Allied Publishers Private Ltd., Bombay, 1961.

30. P.M. Bora, *"Food Administration in India"*, Ajanta Publications, Delhi, 1982.

31. George Boragstron, *"World Food Resources"*, International Text Book Company Ltd., New York, USA, 1973.

32. J.M. Tinley *"South African Food and Agriculture in World War II"*, Food Research Institute, Stanford University, California, 1953.

33. Ross B. TalBot, *"The World Food Problem and U.S. Food Political and Policies; 1972-1976"*, The Lower State University Press, Ames, IOWA, 1977.

34. Hopkins and J. Puchala, *"The Global Political Economy of Food"*, The University of Viston Sin Press, England, 1978.

35. Lamartime Yates, *"Food Land and Manpower in Western Europe"*, Macmillan Company Ltd., London, 1960.

36. B.M. Bhatia, *"India's Food Problem and Policy Since Independence"*, Somaiya Publishing Pvt. Ltd., Bombay, 1970.

37. B.R. Shenoy, *"PL 480 Aid and India Food Problem"*, Affliated East-West Press Pvt. Ltd., New Delhi, 1974.

38. Johnson, *"The Staple Food Economy of Western Tropical Africa"*, Standard University Press, California. 1958.

39. Research and Reference Division (Ed.), *"Food and Civil Supplies in India 1992"*, Ministry of Information and Broadcasting, Government of India, 1993.

40. Peter G. Brown and Henrey Shure (Ed.), *"Food Policy the Responsibility of the United States in the Life and Death Choices"*, The Free Press (A division at Macmillan Publishing Company), New York, 1979.

41. Jos Mooij, *"Food Policy and the Indian State: The Public Distribution System in India"*, Oxford University Press, New Delhi, 1999.

42. Sates Lohkonr and Antony Lanyi, *"Institutions, Incentives and Economic Reforms in India*, Sage Publication, New Delhi.

Journals

1. Bala Krishnan, Pulapre and Ramaswami, Bharat, "Quality of Public Distribution System why it matters", *Economic and Political Weekly*, Vol. 32, No. 4, January 25, 1997, pp. 162-65.

2. Bandyopadhyay, "Food Security and Liberalization" *New Age,* Vol. 45, No. 1, January, 1997, pp. 8-9;.

3. M.L Dantwala, "Agricultural policy: prices and public distribution system: A review" *Indian Journal of Agricultural Economics,* Vol. 48, No. 2, 1993 pp. 173.

4. Div. S. Mahendra, "Food Security: PDS vs. EGS-A tale of two states", *Economic and Political Weekly,* Vol. 31, No. 27, 1996, p, 1752.

5. S. Geetha, and M. H. Suryanarayana, "Revamping PDS Some issues and implications", *Economic and Political Weekly,* Vol. 28, No. 41, 1993 p. 2207.

6. P.S. George, "Public Distribution System food subsidy and production incentives" *Economic and Political Weekly,* Vol. 31, No. 39, 1996, PA, 140.

7. S. Indrakanth, "Coverage and Leakages in PDS in Andhra Pradesh", *Economic and Political Weekly,* Vol. 32, No. 19, 10—May, 1997. pp. 999-1001.

8. S. Indrakanth, "Public Distribution System in Andhra Pradesh with Special Reference to Rice", *Indian Journal of Economics,* Vol. 72, No. 286, 1992 pp. 261.

9. Jagadish Prasad, "Managing Public Distribution Policy. An Analysis the Policy Perspectives", *Indian Journal of Agricultural Economics,* Vol. 47, No. 3, July—September, 1992, pp. 369-70.

10. Jayanthy Selvi, "Public Distribution System in Periyar District", *Tamil Nadu Journal of Cooperation,* Vol. 84, No. 1, April, 1992. pp. 693-700.

11. A.C. Jena, "Public Distribution System and Involvement of Panchayat Raj Institutions, *Kurukshetra* (Annual Number) Vol. 45, No. 1-2, October—November, 1996, pp. 114-17.

12. Jha, Jai Prakash, "Administration of PDS Perspectives, Objectives and Strategy", *Financial Express,* 17, September 1992, pp. 7:3.

13. Kabra, Kamal Nayan and Rao, E.K., "Public Distribution System and Liberation," *Productivity,* Vol. 3, No. 2, July—September, 1992, pp. 229-34.

14. J. Mohan Rao, "Food, Agriculture and Reform", *Economic and Political Weekly,* Vol. 33, No. 29-30, 18, July 1998, pp. 1955-60.

15. Mohan Rao, V., "Revamped Public Distribution", *Yojana,* 15—March, pp. 1992 p. 6-7+.

16. E. Mooij Jos, "Public Distribution System as Safety Net: who is Saved?" *Economic and Political Weekly,* Vol. 29, No. 3, 1994, pp. 119-26.

17. —"Public Distribution System" *Tamil Nadu Journal of Cooperation,* Vol. 84, No. 2, May, 1992 pp. 68-74.

18. —"Public Distribution System: Revamping operational style", *Tamil Nadu Journal of Cooperation,* Vol. 84, No. 5, August, 1992. pp. 265-66.

19. R. Radhakrishna, "Food Trends, Public Distribution System and Food Security Concerns", *Indian Journal of Agricultural Economics,* Vol. 51, No. 1-2, January—June, 1996. pp. 168-83.

20. Ravallion, Martin, "Reforms, Food Prices and Poverty in India. *Economic and Political Weekly,* Vol. 33, No. 1-2, 10—January. 1998, pp. 29-36.

21. Roy, Sunando, "Public Distribution of Cereals: An Alternative Model", *Economic and Political Weekly,* Vol. 27, No. 23, 6—June 1992. pp. 1209-13.

22. Sud, Surinder, "Making Public Distribution System more Effective", *Yojana,* 15—April 1992, pp. 18-20.

23. M.H. Suryanarayana, "Food Security and Calorie Adequacy Across States: Implications for Reform", *Journal of Indian School of Political Economy,* Vol. 8, No. 2, April-June 1996, pp. 203-65.

24. M.H Suryanarayana, "PDS Reform and Scope for Commodity Based Targeting", *Economic and Political Weekly,* Vol. 30, No. 13, 1995, pp. 687-95.

25. Swami Nathan Madhura, "Food Security in India: A Village View of the Public Distribution System in Maharashtra", *Indian Journal of Agricultural Economics*, Vol. 51, No. 4, October—December, 1996, pp. 683-684.

26. "Structural Adjustment: Food Security and System of Public Distribution of Food", *Economic and Political Weekly*, Vol. 31, No. 26, 1996, pp. 1665-1667.

27. R. Thamarajakshi, "Economic Reforms and State Intervention in Foodgrain Market. *Economic and Political Weekly*, Vol. 32, No. 30, July 1997 pp. 1894-1900.

28. Timhang, "Globalisation Challenges Food Security", *Frontier*, Vol. 29, No. 125-26, 25, January, 1997 pp. 12-14.

29. G. Viswanathan, "Effective Public Distribution System in Tamil Nadu," *Tamil Nadu, Journal of Cooperation*, Vol. 85, No. 2, May 1993, pp. 9-13.

30. —"Public Distribution System: A Social Security", *Tamil Nadu Journal of Cooperation*, Vol. 85, No. 2, May, 1993, pp. 3-8.

31. Moni Nag, "Beliefs and Practices About Food During Pregnancy", *Economic and Political Weekly*, Vol. XXIX, No. 37, September-10, 1994, pp. 2427-37.

32. Madhura Swaminathan, "Revamped Public Distribution System; A Field Report from Maharashtra", *Economic and Political Weekly*, Vol. XXX, No. 36, September-9, 1995, p. 2230.

33. KPK, "Growing Food Deficit", *Economic and Political Weekly*, Vol. XXII, No. 18, March-2, 1987, pp. 773-74.

34. Raghbendra Jha and et al, "Real Consumption Levels and Public Distribution System in India", *Economic and Political Weekly*, Vol. XXXIV, No. 15, April 10-16, 1999, pp. 919-27.

35. J.V. Meenakshi, "How Important Are Change in Taste; A State Level Analysis of Food Demand", *Economic and Political Weekly,* Vol. XXXI, No. 50, December 14, 1996, pp. 3265-69.

36. Utsa Patnaik, "Export—oriented Agricultural and Food Security in Developing Countries and India", *Economic and Political Weekly,* Vol. XXXI, Nos. 35, 36, and 37 Special Number, September, 1996, pp. 2429-49.

37. Jayati Ghosh and et al, "Using Food Stocks Productively", *Economic and Political Weekly,* Vol. XXXI, No. 21, May—25, 1996, pp. 1235-37.

38. Kaushik Basu, "Food for Work Programmes; Beyond Roads that Get Washed Away", *Economic and Political Weekly,* Vol. XVI, No. 1 and 2, January 3-10, 1981, pp. 37-40.

39. JM, "Food Exports and Requirement", *Economic and Political Weekly,* Vol. XXIX, No. 35, August 27, 1994, pp. 2261-64.

40. P.C. Bansil, "Demand for Foodgrains by 2020", *Economic and Political Weekly,* Vol. XXXIII, No. 10, March 7-13, 1998 pp. 546-548.

41. S. Mahedradev, "Growth and Instability in Foodgrains Production an Inter-state Analysis", *Economic and Political Weekly,* Vol. XXII, No. 39, September 26, 1987, pp. 82-83.

42. M.H. Suryanarayana, "Urban Bias in PDS", *Economic and Political Weekly,* Vol. XXIX, No. 9, February 26, 1994, pp. 510-512.

43. S. Mahendra Dev, "Economics Reforms and the Rural poor", *Economic and Political Weekly",* Vol. XXX, No. 33, August 19, 1995, pp. 2085-2088.

44. Madhura Swaminathan, "Food for Profit, *Economic and Political Weekly",* Vol. XXXIV, No. 13, March 27, April 2, 1997, pp. 747-755.

45. M.H. Suranarayana, "Food Security; Misconceived policies", *Economic and Political Weekly,* Vol. XXXI, No. 9, July 20, 1996, pp. 1935-1936.

46. Vandana Shiva, "Geopolitics of Food, America's use of Food as a Weapon", *Economic and Political Weekly,* Vol. XXIII, No. 18 April 1-30, 1998, pp. 881-882.

47. Y.L. Das, "Public Distribution System: A study of Bihar", *Southern Economist,* February-1, 1993, pp. 15-17.

48. N. Durairaj, "Rationale of Foodgrains Procurement Policy; Some Contentions Issues", *Southern Economist,* March 1, 1984, pp. 14-16.

49. Sankar Majumder and Purnendu Sekhar Das, "Identifying Surplus Foodgrain, Areas: A Different Approach", *Economic Affairs,* Vol. 38, Quarter 2, June 1993, pp. 89-96.

50. Shahnawaz Malik, "Targeted Food Subsidy as a Short-term Measure for Rural Poverty Alleviation in Pakistan", *Economic Affairs,* Vol. 38, Quarter 1, March 1993, pp. 57-60.

51. B. Dadgostar, "Integrated Approach to Demand Analysis for Food in Thailand", *Economic Affairs,* Vol. 32, Quarter 3, September, 1987, pp. 153-163.

52. R.C. Oberoi and K.K. Raina, "Growth and Diversification of Foodgrains in Himachal Pradesh", *Economic Affairs,* Vol. 36, Quarter. 3, September 1991, pp. 155-160.

53. Thomaskutty Abraham, "Wheat Export: Wheat Export Doubles the Trouble", *Industrial Economist,* 30 April-14 May 1994, p. 46.

54. P.C. Anil Kumar, "Public Distribution System in Doldrums", *Indian Journal of Marketing* Vol., No. 5 and 6, January-February, 1981, pp. 23-24 and 32.

55. A. Sankaraiah, "Public Distribution System, An Empirical Assessment", *Indian Journal of Marketing,* Vol. XIV, No. 5, January 1984, pp. 3-6 and 11.

56. R.S. Khare, "The Issue of Right to Food Among the Hindus: Notes and Comments", *Contributions to Indian Sociology,* Vol. 32, No. 2, July-December, 1998, pp. 253-277.

57. Partha Pratim Mitra, "Economics of Food Security; The Indian Context", *Social Action,* Vol. 46, No. 3, July—September 1996, pp. 278-294.

58. U. Upadhyay, "Inflation, Food Security and Public Distribution System", *Social Action,* Vol. 46, No. 3, July-September, 1996, pp. 296-308.

59. V.S Vyas, "Diversification in Agriculture: Concept, Rationale and Approaches, *Indian Journal of Agricultural Economics,* Vol. 51, No. 4, October—December, 1996, pp. 636-651.

60. Ramesh Chand, "Diversification through Highvalue Crops in Western Himalayan Region; Evidence from Himachal Pradesh", *Indian Journal of Agricultural Economics,* Vol. 51, No. 4, October—December, 1996, pp. 652-663.

61. Praduman Kumar and V.C. Mathur; "Structural Changes in the Demand for Food in India", *Indian Journal of Agricultural Economics,* Vol. 51, No. 4, October—December, 1996, pp. 664-673.

62. K.J.S. Satyasai and K.U. Viswanathan, Diversification at Indian Agriculture and Food Security, *Indian Journal of Agricultural Economics,* Vol. 51, No. 4, October-December 1996, pp. 674-679.

63. John Cathie and Roland Hermann, "The Southern African Customs Union, Cereal price policy in South Africa, and food Security in Botswana", *The Journal of*

Development Studies, Vol. 24, No. 3, April 1998, pp. 395-414.

64. Sudhakar Tripathy and M.V. Srinivasa Gowda, "Sources of Variability of Foodgrains Production in Orissa", *Indian Journal of Agricultural Economics",* Vol. 50, No. 4, October-December 1995.

65. Dhayanantha Jha, "Rapporteur's Report on Diversitication of Agriculture and Food Security in the Context of New Economic policy", *Indian Journal of Agricultural Economics,* Vol. 51, No. 4, October-December 1996, pp. 829-832.

66. Ajit Kumar Ghose, "Food Supply and Starvation: A study of Famines with Reference to the Indian Sub-Continent", *Oxford Economic Papers,* Vol. 34, No. 2, July 1982, pp. 368-338.

67. C. Kailasam and et al, "A study on the effect of subsidy on Household food consumption in Western Tamil Nadu", *Artha Vijana,* Vol. 35, No. 2, June, 1993, pp. 150-159.

68. G.K. Mitra, "Demand for Cereals in Seventh Plan," *Artha Vijana,* Vol. 28, No. 4, December 1986, pp. 386-394.

69. Tripta Desai, "Indo-American Wheat Negotiations of 1950-1951", *The Indian Political Science Review,* Vol. 2, July 1975, pp. 118-151.

70. John W. Mellor and Richard H. Adams JR, "Feeding the under Developed World; Chemical Technology is Crucial in alleviating poverty and hunger", *Chemical & Engineering News,* April 1-23, 1985, pp. 32-39.

71. Dayanatha Jha, "Employment For Poverty Reduction and Food Security", *Indian Journal of Agricultural Economics* Vol. 52, No. 4, October-December 1997 pp. 814-819.

72. C.T. Kurien, "Competitive Strategy Analysis in the Food System", *Indian Journal of Agricultural Economics,* Vol. 52, No. 4, October-December 1997, pp. 814-819.

73. Harish Damodaran, "FCI's logistics of foodgrain movement mind-boggling space and time constraints", *Business Line,* May 17, 1999, p. 4.

74. I. Satya Sundaram, "Facets of Food Economy of India", *Southern Economist,* Vol. 29, No. 20, February 15, 1991, p. 23.

75. A.N. Pandey, "Growing Enough Food for India's Millions", *Southern Economist,* February 1, 1982.

76. Reji and D. Nair, "Population Growth and Food Availability", *Third Concept,* Vol. 12, No. 136, June 1998, pp. 54-57.

77. T.R. Gurumoorthy, "Public Distribution System: A Boon to People Below Poverty Line", *Third Concept,* Vol. 11, No. 128-129, October-November 97, pp. 63-65.

78. Harold alderman and Kathy Lindert, "The Potential and Limitations of Self-Targeted Food Subsidies", *The World Bank Research Observer,* Vol. 13, No. 2, August pp. 213-229.

79. Partha Gangopadhay, *"Food Speculation and Strategic Monetary Management in a Developing Economy"*. The Indian Economic Journal, Vol. 45, No. 4, April-June 97-98, pp. 145-149.

80. V. Vasudeva Rao, *"Role of PDS in Food Security"*, Social Welfare Vol. 46, No. 6, September 1999, pp. 7-10.

81. Radhakrishna Rao, *"An alternate PDS of Food Security in Telegram"*, Social Welfare, Vol. 46, No. 6, September 1999 pp. 11-12.

82. Archana Sinha, *"Empowering Women for Food Security"*. Social Welfare, Vol. 46, No. 6, September 1999, pp. 3-6.

83. C. Shanmugam, *"Co-operatives and Public Distribution System"*, The Tamil Nadu Journal of Co-operation, Vol. 91, No. 6, September 1999, pp. 16-22.

84. P.V. Srinivasan, Shikha Jha, *"Food Security through Price Stabilisation: Buffer Stocks vs. Variable Levis"*, Economic and Political Weekly, Vol. XXIV, No. 46 and 47, November 20, 1999 pp. 3299-3304.

85. Daman Prakash, *"Food Security Issues, WTO and Agricultural Co-operatives in Asia"*, Indian Co-operative Review, Vol. XXXVI, No. 2, October 1998, pp. 95-101.

86. Peter G. Brown and Hency Shur (Ed.), *"Food Security Issues, WTO and Agriculture Co-operatives in Asia"*, Indian Co-operative Review, Vol. XXXVI, No. 2, October 1998, pp. 95-101.

87. S. Geetha, and Surya Narayanan M.H., *"Revamping PDS some Issues and Implication,* Economic and Political Weekly, October 9, 1993, pp. 3307-2213.

88. R. Siddappan, *"Public Distribution System: A case study of Gulmaged District in Karnataka"*, Southern Economist, Vol. 30, No. 19, February 1992, pp. 13-14.

89. P.S. George, *"Food Security in South Asia"*, Economic and Political Weekly, April 1994, pp. 1092-94.

90. Mahendra Dev, S. *"Is PDS Reform and Scope for Community Based Targeting"*, Economic and Political Weekly, October 1991, pp. 2357-60.

91. M.H. Surya Narayana, *"PDS Reform and Scope for Community based targeting"*, Economic and Political Weekly, October, pp. 2357-60.

92. Kurian Lanki, *"Ending Food Subsidies Nutritional Welfare and Budgetary Effect"*, The World Bank Economic Review, 33, pp. 395-408.

93. K.S. Krishanaswamy, *"Agricultural Development under the New Economic Regime,* Economic and Political Weekly",", Vol. 26 No. 26, June, 1994. pp. 5-7.

94. C.H. Hanumantha Rao, *"Liberalisation and Agriculture"*, National Bank News Review, Vol. 10, No. 3, July, 1994. pp.38-41.

95. Ashish Bose, *"Population, PDS and Planning in Madhya Pradesh"*. Financial Express, July 1993, pp. 7.

96. Bandila K. Padha, *"Importance of food and Percapita Availability of foodgrain in India"*, Southern Economist, April 1991. pp 9-20.

97. Beaseaw F.F, *"Among is Assessment on Food Subsidy"*, Financial Express, March 1993, pp.11.

98. *Food Buffer Comprehensive"*, Financial Express, July 1993, pp. 11.

99. K.T. Dilli, *"Food and Nutritional Security"*, Third Concept, February 1995, pp. 39-42.

100. Krishna Rao, 1. YR, *"An Experiment in Food Security"* Economic and Political Weekly, Vol. 28, No 37, September 1993, pp 1911-1914.

101. Kuriya Patticle C and Green C, *"A Cooperative Society Analysis of Food Security in Developing Countries"*, Journal of Development Studies, No. 18, January, 1982, pp 185-204.

102. Murali Dhasan Sukumar, *"Food Subsidies, IMF Prescription could spell Troubles"*, Economic and Political Weekly, Vol. 26, No. 17, April 1991. pp. 1083-85.

103. A.N, Sharma and Ashok Gulati, *"Subsidising Agriculture"*, Economic and Political Weekly, Vol. 27, No. 39, September 1992, pp. 106-115.

104. M. Raghvan, *"Some aspects of Growth and Distribution of Rice in India"*, Social Scientist, Vol. 27, No. 5-6, May-June, 1999. pp 62-85.

105. N. Baskaran. (Ed). *"Advisory Committees for the better functioning of PDS"*, The Tamil Nadu Journal of Co-operation, Vol. 89, No. 6, September 1997.

106. N.Baskaran Ed, "Public Distribution system Computerised Bogus card would be Eliminated fully Raised Quantum of Rice supplied to card holders Now only," The Tamil Nadu Journal of Co-operation, Vol. 89, No. 5, August 1997.

107. Baskaran Ed, "Intensive cheek in Fair Price Shops Continued Large Number of Bogus Cards Unerthened", The Tamil Nadu Journal of Co-operation, Vol. 89, No. 5, August 1997.

108. K. Baskaran Ed, "5000 New Ration Shops to be Opened in Tamil Nadu, The Tamil Nadu Journal of Co-operation, Vol. 89, No. 4, July 1997.

109. K.N. Nanjundan, "Cooperation Ministers Suggestion to Streamline the PDS", The Tamil Nadu Journal of Co-operation, Vol. 88, and No. 12, March 1997.

110. K.N. Nanjundan, *"PDS Review Meeting with Co-operative officials"*, The Tamil Nadu Journal of Co-operation, Vol. 88, No. 12, March 1997.

111. L. Sitharasenan, (Ed) *"K.N. Nehru Minister for Food Cooperation* in the Legislative Assembly", The Tamil Nadu Journal of Cooperation, Vol. 89, No. 2, May 1997.

112. L. Sitharasenan, *"World Wise Fair Price Shops in Kumbakonam"*, The Tamil Nadu Journal of Co-operation, Vol. 89, and No. 2, May 1997.

113. L. Sitharasenan (Ed) *"Special Projects to Develop Tamil Nadu by food Department"*, The Tamil Nadu Journal of Co-operation, Vol. 89, No. 2, May 1997.

114. Josmooij, *"Dillemmas in Food Policy, About Institutional Contradictions and Vested Interests"*, Economic and Political Weekly, Vol. XXXIV, No. 52, December 25, 1999. pp. A114-A120.

115. Madhura Swaminathan, *"Understanding the cost of the Food Co-operation of India"*, Economic and Political

Weekly, Vol. XXXIV, No. 52, Dec. 25, 1999. pp. A121-132.

116. Editor, *"Poor Programme"*, The Hindu, Vol. 7. No. 63, March 4, 2000.

117. T.R. Gurumurthy, *"Sugar Import"*, Third Concept, Vol. 13, No. 156, February 2000.

118. S. Sahul Hameed, *"Foodgrains Production"*, Third Concept, Vol. 13, No. 156 February, 2000

119. Editorials, *"Minister Hints at Revamping of PDS"*, The Hindu, October- 23, 1999.

120. R.S Dhanajayam, and Anbumani- V. *"Public Distribution System and the Indian Experience"* Southern Economist, January-15 1981.

121. Person Kumar and Punamkumari Verma *"Public Distribution System in India; At a Glance"* Southern Economist, May 1. 1995.

122. D.K. Nauraiyal and Tradti Tiwari, *"Public Distribution System, Need for Restricting"*. The Cooperator, May 15, 1987, Vol., No. 22.

123. B.J. Azad *"States Should Expand Public Distribution System"*. The Cooperator, June, 1, Vol. XX, No. 23.

124. A. Shankarain and R. Sudarshan *"Public Distribution System"* "An Empirical Assessment". Indian Journal of Marketing, Vol. XIV, and No. 5, January 1984.

125. Srivastava, K.B., *"Management of Public Distribution in India"*. Journal of Rural Development, No. 4. September 1985.

126. B.J. Heerjee, *"Public Distribution of Consumer Articles"*, The Cooperator, Vol. XX, No. 10. November 15, 1983.

127. Suneep Khanna, *"Problems of Procurement and Distribution"* Kurukshetra, Vol. XXIX, No. 18, June 16, 1981.

128. Srivastava, S.C., *"Public Distribution System and Welfare in India"* Southern Economist, May. 15, 1983.

129. Sharma, K.D. and Mathu N.D., *"Public Distribution System under Sixth Plan"*, The Cooperator, Vol., No. 15, February 1, 1982.

130. Tapeshware Sing, Consumer Cooperatives and Public Distribution Systems, Tamil Nadu Journal of Cooperation, May 1979. pp 453-54.

131. S. Arunachalam and P. Krishna, *"Public Distribution System"*, Tamil Nadu Journal of Cooperation, May 92.

132. I. Satya Sundram, *"PDS Evalution"*, Indian Consumer Cooperator, Vol. 22, October-December 19, 1995.

133. M.S. Alisagar, *"Role of Cooperatives in the PDS"*, Tamil Nadu Journal of Cooperation, May 1979. pp. 455-459.

134. R.S. Umre, *"Rural Cooperatives and PDS"*, Tamil Nadu Journal Cooperation, Vol. 20. May, 1979.

135. M.H, Suryanarayana, *"Reform and its Human Face"*, The Hindu, 16th Feb. 1996. pp. 12.

136. Martin Ravallion, *"Reform, Food Prices and Poverty in India,"* Economic and Political Weekly, Vol. XXXIII No. 1-3, January 6-10-1998.

137. Biksam K. Pattaraik, *"Rural Poverty and PDS"* Yojana Vol. 41, No. 11, November 1997. pp. 37-42.

138. Gargi Parsai, "PDS Rice Price to be Hiked, The Hindu, 9th October. 1999.

139. Editor, *"No Change in PDS Price"*, The Hindu, Sunday October 16, 1999. p. 3.

140. Gargi Parsari, *"Unpolished Rice for TPDS Likely"*, The Hindu, 4th November. pp. 13.

141. S.S Barnala, *"Issue Prices of PDS Wheat Rice to Stay"*, The Hindu, 23rd February 1999.

142. Editor, *"Panel Recommdends Increase in TPDS Quota"*, The Hindu, 27th 3 April, 1999.

143. Gargi Parsai, *"Hike Likely in PDS Wheat Quota for Poor"*, The Hindu, Wednesday May, 1999, P. 15.

144. Editor, *"The PDS under Panchayats"*, The Hindu, 7th July 1999.

145. Gargi Parsai, *"I like in Price of PDS Essential's on the anvil"*, The Hindu, 28th January 1999.

146. Gargi Parsai, *"TPPS remains an unfinished task"*, The Hindu, 10th December 1997.

147. S. Mahendra dev, *"Public Distribution System: Impact on Poor and options for Reform"*, Economic and Political Weekly, Vol. XXXIII. No. 35, August 29, September 4. 1998. pp. 2285-2290.

148. Editor, *TANWA-Trained Women Man Operate Ration Shop*, The Hindu, 28th April 1999.

149. Editor, *"Ration Rice, Wheat Prices up"*, The Hindu, 29th January 1999.

150. Editor, *"Small Hike in Price of PDS Kerosene Likely"*, The Hindu, 29th January 1999.

151. Editor, *"Ex-factory Heavy Sugar Price to be Liked Soon,"* The Hindu, December 21. 1999.

152. Editor, *"CPI (M) Suggests Monopoly Procurement of Paddy,"* The Hindu, 20th December 1998.

153. Editor, *"Govt. Plans Survey to Check Ration Card details"*, The Hindu, 26th January, 1999.

154. Editor, *"Computer Network for PDS"*, The Hindu, 20th January, 1999.

155. Editor, "Subsidy on PDS Rice Nearing Rs. 1500 crores, The Hindu, 26th January, 1999.

156. Editor, *"Grain Price act helps State Avoid Subsidy,"* The Hindu, 3rd February 1999.

157. Editor, *"PDS Price Hike puts State Government in a fix"*, The Hindu, 1st February 1999.

158. Gargi Parsai, *"TPDS Rice Norms Proposal Returned"*, The Hindu, 3rd, March 1999.

159. Editor, *"Fall in PDS Rice off take"*, The Hindu, 11th April 1999.

160. Editor, "Roll-back of Foodgrains Price Hike Ruled out, The Hindu, 1st February, 1999.

161. C. Ram Manohar Reddy, *"The Issue of Subsidies,"* The Hindu, 6th February 1999.

162. Editor, *"Monopoly Procurement for Samba"*, The Hindu, 22nd. December 1998.

163. Editor, "TNCSC Unlikely to Reach Procurement Target, The Hindu, 12th March, 1999.

164. Deepak Kumar Nishra, "Trends in Foodgrains Production: Implication for Future, Southern Economist, Vol. 36, No. 6, 1997. pp 17-19.

165. Editor, "Food and Nutritional Security, Southern Economist, Vol. 36, No. 12 October 15, 1997. pp. 1-2.

166. I Mohan Rao, "Food Prices and Rural Poverty Liberalisation with out Pain? Economic and Political Weekly, Vol. XXXIII, No. 14, April 4, 1998. pp. 799-800.

167. Special Correspondent, "Open Sale to Wheat Scheme Liberalised, The Hindu, August, 10. 1999.

168. Special Correspondent, "MSP for Paddy Inadequate Badal, The Hindu, July 21, 1999.

169. Vandana Shiva, "The Wheat Opportunity in India, The Hindu, July, 19, 1999.

170. S. Swaminathan, Embassassing Surfeit in Wheat, The Hindu, May 14, 1999.

171. Pulapre Balakrishnan, Food Security and Panchayat Raj, The Hindu, July 12, 1999.

172. Special Correspondent," Wheat Procurement: FCI Sets new record, The Hindu, May 12, 1999.

173. CRR, "Food Security and Insecurity, The Hindu, October 21, 1999. pp. 19.

174. Gail Omvedt, Rotting food, The Hindu, Oct 23, 1999.

175. A. Vaidyanathan, "On Subsidies-I" The Hindu, September 1, 1997. pp. 12.

176. Jacques Diouf, Food Security towards Lunges free Century weak lines of Local Production, access, The Hindu, May 5, 1999.

177. Ananta and Path, "Social Net Works and Food Security in Rural Karnataka", Economic and Political Weekly, Vol. XXXII-No. 15 April 12, 1997.

178. Editor, "Food Security in Jeopardy, Monthly Public Opinion Surveys", Vol. XIII No. 7, April 1, 1997. pp. 5-6.

179. G. Suryanarayana, "Public Distribution System- An Assessment", Southern Economist, Vol. 16, No. 10, September 15, 1977.

180. Ragbendra Jha, "The Determinants of the Price of Food in India", Indian Journal of Applied Economics, Vol. 6, No. 1, 1997. pp. 75-81.

181. Paratha Gangopadhyay, "Food Speculation and Strategic Monetary Management in a Developing Economy," The Indian economic Journal, Vol. 45, No. 4, April-June 1997-98. pp. 51-52.

182. P.V. Rajeev, "Poverty and Food Security," Third Concept, Vol. 11, No. 121, March 1997, pp. 145-149.

183. Ravi Kanbur, Machael Keen and et al, "Labour Supply and Targeting in Poverty Alleviation Programmes,"

The World Bank Economic Review, Vol. 8, No. 2, May 1994.

184. Shahna Waz Malik, "Targeted Food Subsidy is a Short term Measure for Rural Poverty in Pakistan", Economic Affairs, Vol. 38, Qly 2, January-March 1993. pp. 57-60.

185. Saini A.S, K.D. Shasma, and et al, "Foodgrains Production, Demand and Prices in India", Indian Journal of Agricultural Marketing, Vol. 8, and No. 2 July-December 1994. pp. 221-230.

186. Prabhu Nath Sing," Supply Management Through Public Distribution System, Southern Economist, May 15, Vol. 18, 1979.

187. Gopal Krishnan, "Public Distribution of Foodgrains Role of Co-operatives", Co-operative New Digest, Vol. XXIV.

188. Editor, Revamping Public Distribution System", Southern Economist July 2, 1986.

189. P.S. George, "Food Security in South Asia", Economic and Political Weekly, Vol. 28, No. 18, April 1994. pp. 1092-94.

190. V.M. Rao, Beyond surpluses, "Food Security in Changing Concept, Economic and Political Weekly", Vol. 30, No. 14, January 1995. pp. 215-19.

191. V.A. Vasudevaraju, "Welfare of Market", New Time Observer, 26th October 1998. pp. 2.

192. Editor, "Public Distribution System Price up in Tamil Nadu", The Hindu, October 12, 1999. pp. 2.